POEMS AND SONGS OF THE CIVIL WAR

★ ★ ★ ★ ★ ★ ★ ★ ★ ★ ★

POEMS AND SONGS OF THE CIVIL WAR

★ ★ ★ ★ ★ ★ ★ ★ ★ ★ ★ ★ ★ ★ ★ ★ ★

Edited by Lois Hill

THE FAIRFAX PRESS
New York

First published in 1990 by The Fairfax Press, distributed by Outlet Book Company, Inc., a Random House Company, 225 Park Avenue South, New York, New York 10003.

Printed and bound in the United States of America

Library of Congress Cataloging-in-Publication Data
Poems and songs of the Civil War / edited by Lois Hill.
    p. cm.
  ISBN 0-517-69918-4
    1. United States—History—Civil War, 1861–1865—Poetry. 2. United States—History—Civil War, 1861–1865—Songs and music—Texts. 3. Songs, English—United States—Texts. 4. War-songs—United States—Texts. 5. American poetry—19th century. 6. War poetry, American. I. Hill, Lois.
PS595.C55P64 1990
811'.4080358—dc20
                                                                89-78424
                                                                CIP

8 7 6 5 4 3 2 1

CONTENTS

★ ★ ★ ★ ★ ★

v

GETTYSBURG

THE END OF THE STRUGGLE

BROTHERHOOD

FAMOUS LYRICS

SONGS OF THE CIVIL WAR

INTRODUCTION

* * * * * * *

The poems and songs of the Civil War era are gripping and powerful. From the secession of South Carolina and the opening battle at Fort Sumter to Lee's surrender at Appomattox and Lincoln's assassination, this wealth of literature records a remarkable period in American history from an urgent, contemporary perspective.

Moved by the currents of the divergent principles and needs that tore the nation in half, northern and southern authors alike express their horror at the bloodshed and sacrificed lives. In these patriotic and sentimental works, they tell tales of heroes and daring deeds, find solace in memory, and commemorate their dead. Finally, after the bitter end of the war, they assume the burdens of the peace and begin to reconstruct the nation. In the voices of these poets—speaking, writing, singing—lies the full spectrum of the history and emotions of the Civil War.

This anthology owes its form and much of its content to a work published some forty-seven years after the war had ended: *Poetry and Eloquence of Blue and Gray,* volume nine of the ten-volume series entitled *The Photographic History of the Civil War.* One of the original editors of the *Photographic History* series, W. P. Trent, developed a vehement dislike of the poetry selected for his volume by Dudley H. Miles, so much so that he wrote in a curiously negative *Foreword* to the book:

> In literature as in life it will not do to assume unreservedly that the fittest will survive, and then to argue that because something has survived, it has proved its fitness. It will be gathered from the tone of these remarks that I do not think that much of the poetry Dr. Miles has included, suitable though it is for the present work, would find a place in a volume edited with an exigence equal to that manifested by the late Mr. Palgrave in his "Golden Treasury."

The value of this poetry is as much historical as it is literary. Many minor or one-time authors contributed their manifold talents to the poetry of this period; if a poet fails to escape the snares of rhyme, his blood-and-thunder verses still depict the raging battle in which he himself fought or to which he was a witness. Trent's comparison is neither justified nor warranted, but one hopes that his judgmental presence is assuaged by the current and judicious addition of certain verses, in particular Walt Whitman's splendid poetry. Another literary voice totally neglected at that time and now represented is that of Herman Melville, who was not rescued from literary limbo until the decade following the publication of the *Photographic History* series.

For this edition the "eloquence" (speeches and essays of the period) and photographs have been eliminated, poems added and deleted to complete revised sections, and introductory remarks supplied for each chapter. Birth and death dates for the poets, when known, are given at the head of their first poem appearing in the volume. The poetry is divided into thematic sections that run sequentially from the beginning of the war through the beginning of Reconstruction.

Poems and Songs of the Civil War is a unique volume in which the fierce patriotism and high emotions aroused in a nation divided and at war with itself run as thickly as the blood on the battlefields. It is the voice of America singing in joy and sorrow and it is the literary heritage of the Civil War.

SEPARATION

On December 20, 1860, the South Carolina legislature voted to secede from the United States of America. In the following months, six other southern states chose to withdraw from the Union: Mississippi, Florida, Alabama, Georgia, Louisiana, and Texas. Four more—Virginia, Arkansas, North Carolina, and Tennessee—would join the Confederate States of America after the Union garrison at Fort Sumter, South Carolina, fell to the Confederacy on April 12, 1861, in the opening battle of the Civil War.

Oliver Wendell Holmes' poem, "Brother Jonathan's Lament for Sister Caroline," was written literally on the eve of the Civil War. Dated March 25, 1861, this striking prophecy of war before war had begun ("O Caroline, Caroline, child of the sun, there are battles with Fate that can never be won!") predates by only four days President Abraham Lincoln's March 29th order for Union reinforcements to be sent to help defend Fort Sumter in Charleston Harbor. Holmes is among the more prominent literary figures of the poets in this volume. Born in Cambridge, Massachusetts, he graduated from Harvard at the age of twenty, and by twenty-one had became famous for his poem "Old Ironsides." Poet, humorist, physician, and Harvard Law School professor, Holmes gained national recognition for his series of entertaining and intelligent essays, "The Autocrat of the Breakfast Table," published by *Atlantic Monthly* in 1857. In 1861, at the time of "Brother Jonathan's Lament for Sister Caroline," he was a nationally recognized poet.

In sharp contrast to the style of "Sister Caroline," Walt Whitman's "Eighteen Sixty-One" hits the reader with the strong, clean lines of the nation's call to arms in the first year of the war. Whitman's voice is startlingly modern; stripped bare of the sentimentalism and rhyme of the period, his poetry has a palpable immediacy and an enduring

2

presence. Whitman saw little direct action in the war; he served as an army orderly in the Washington hospitals after nursing his brother, who had been wounded in the battle of Fredericksburg. From these Civil War experiences came the book of poetry entitled *Drum Taps,* which he himself described as "a little book containing life's darkness and blood-dropping wounds and psalms of the dead."

The two concluding poems in this section, "Charleston" by Henry Timrod and "To the South" by James Maurice Thompson, do not relate directly to the beginning of the war. They do, however, express the very distinct personality of the South, and are therefore included under the heading "Separation." Timrod, who was born in Charleston, was an army correspondent whose lyrics set thousands of Southern hearts on fire. His famous poem was written in the calm preceding the attack on Charleston by Admiral Samuel F. Dupont on April 17, 1863. Thompson's "To the South" celebrates Savannah, which was virtually untouched during four long years of war until its devastation by William Tecumseh Sherman's troops in December 1864.

BROTHER JONATHAN'S LAMENT FOR SISTER CAROLINE

Oliver Wendell Holmes (1809–1894)

★ ★ ★ ★ ★ ★ ★

She has gone,—she has left us in passion and pride,—
Our stormy-browed sister, so long at our side!
She has torn her own star from our firmament's glow,
And turned on her brother the face of a foe!

O Caroline, Caroline, child of the sun,
We can never forget that our hearts have been one,—
Our foreheads both sprinkled in Liberty's name,
From the fountain of blood with the finger of flame!

You were always too ready to fire at a touch;
But we said: "She is hasty,—she does not mean much."
We have scowled when you uttered some turbulent threat;
But Friendship still whispered: "Forgive and forget!"

Has our love all died out? Have its altars grown cold?
Has the curse come at last which the fathers foretold?
Then Nature must teach us the strength of the chain
That her petulant children would sever in vain.

They may fight till the buzzards are gorged with their spoil,—
Till the harvest grows black as it rots in the soil,
Till the wolves and the catamounts troop from their caves,
And the shark tracks the pirate, the lord of the waves:

In vain is the strife! When its fury is past,
Their fortunes must flow in one channel at last,
As the torrents that rush from the mountains of snow
Roll mingled in peace through the valleys below.

Our Union is river, lake, ocean, and sky;
Man breaks not the medal when God cuts the die!
Though darkened with sulphur, though cloven with steel,
The blue arch will brighten, the waters will heal!

O Caroline, Caroline, child of the sun,
There are battles with Fate that can never be won!
The star-flowering banner must never be furled,
For its blossoms of light are the hope of the world!

Go, then, our rash sister! afar and aloof,—
Run wild in the sunshine away from our roof;
But when your heart aches and your feet have grown sore,
Remember the pathway that leads to our door!

EIGHTEEN SIXTY-ONE
Walt Whitman (1819–1892)

★ ★ ★ ★ ★ ★

Arm'd year—year of the struggle,
No dainty rhymes or sentimental love verses for you,
    terrible year,
Not you as some pale poetling seated at a desk
    lisping cadenzas piano,
But as a strong man erect, clothed in blue clothes,
    advancing, carrying a rifle on your shoulder,
With well-gristled body and sunburnt face and hands,
    with a knife in the belt at your side,
As I heard you shouting loud, your sonorous voice
    ringing across the continent,
Your masculine voice, O year, as rising amid
    the great cities,
Amid the men of Manhattan I saw you as one
    of the workmen, the dwellers in Manhattan,
Or with large steps crossing the prairies out
    of Illinois and Indiana,
Rapidly crossing the West with springy gait
    and descending the Alleghanies,
Or down from the great lakes or in Pennsylvania,
    or on deck along the Ohio river,
Or southward along the Tennessee or Cumberland rivers,
    or at Chattanooga on the mountain top,
Saw I your gait and saw I your sinewy limbs
    clothed in blue, bearing weapons, robust year,

Heard your determin'd voice launch'd forth
     again and again,
Year that suddenly sang by the mouths of the
     round-lipp'd cannon,
I repeat you, hurrying, crashing, sad, distracted
     year.

CHARLESTON

Henry Timrod (1828–1867)

* * * * * * *

Calm as that second summer which precedes
　　The first fall of the snow,
In the broad sunlight of heroic deeds,
　　The city bides the foe.

As yet, behind their ramparts, stern and proud,
　　Her bolted thunders sleep,—
Dark Sumter, like a battlemented cloud,
　　Looms o'er the solemn deep.

No Calpe frowns from lofty cliff or scaur
　　To guard the holy strand;
But Moultrie holds in leash her dogs of war
　　Above the level sand.

And down the dunes a thousand guns lie couched,
　　Unseen, beside the flood,—
Like tigers in some Orient jungle crouched,
　　That wait and watch for blood.

Meanwhile, through streets still echoing with trade,
　　Walk grave and thoughtful men,
Whose hands may one day wield the patriot's blade
　　As lightly as the pen.

And maidens, with such eyes as would grow dim
  Over a bleeding hound,
Seem each one to have caught the strength of him
  Whose sword she sadly bound.

Thus girt without and garrisoned at home,
  Day patient following day,
Old Charleston looks from roof and spire and dome,
  Across her tranquil bay.

Ships, through a hundred foes, from Saxon lands
  And spicy Indian ports,
Bring Saxon steel and iron to her hands,
  And summer to her courts.

But still, along yon dim Atlantic line,
  The only hostile smoke
Creeps like a harmless mist above the brine,
  From some frail floating oak.

Shall the spring dawn, and she, still clad in smiles,
  And with an unscathed brow,
Rest in the strong arms of her palm-crowned isles,
  As fair and free as now?

We know not; in the temple of the Fates
  God has inscribed her doom:
And, all untroubled in her faith, she waits
  The triumph or the tomb.

TO THE SOUTH
James Maurice Thompson (1844–1901)

★ ★ ★ ★ ★ ★ ★

O subtle, musky, slumbrous clime!
   O swart, hot land of pine and palm,
Of fig, peach, guava, orange, lime,
   And terebinth and tropic balm!
Land where our Washington was born,
When truth in hearts of gold was worn;
Mother of Marion, Moultrie, Lee,
Widow of fallen chivalry!
No longer sadly look behind,
But turn and face the morning wind,
And feel sweet comfort in the thought:
     "With each fierce battle's sacrifice
     I sold the wrong at awful price,
  And bought the good; but knew it not."

Cheer up! Reach out! Breathe in new life!
Brood not on unsuccessful strife
Against the current of the age;
The Highest is thy heritage!
Leave off this death's-head scowl at Fate,
And into thy true heart sink this:
"God loves to walk where Freedom is!"

There is no sweet in dregs and lees;
There is no fruit on girdled trees.
Plant new vineyards, sow new fields,

10

For bread and wine the Future yields;
Out of free soil fresh spathes shall start;
Now is the budding-time of Art!

But hark! O hear! My senses reel!
Some grand presentiment I feel!
A voice of love, bouquet of truth,
The quick sound of the feet of youth!

Lo! from the war-cloud, dull and dense,
    Loyal and chaste and brave and strong,
Comes forth the South with frankincense,
    And vital freshness in her song.
The weight is fallen from her wings;
To find a purer air she springs
Out of the Night into the Morn,
Fair as cotton, sound as corn.

Hold! Shall a Northman, fierce and grim,
With hoary beard and boreal vim,
Thus fling, from some bleak waste of ice,
Frost-crystals of unsought advice
    To those who dwell by Coosa's stream,
Or on dark hummocks plant the cane
Beside the lovely Pontchartrain,
    Or in gay sail-boats drift and dream
Where Caribbean breezes stray
On Pensacola's drowsy bay?

Not so! I am a Southerner;
I love the South; I dared for her
To fight from Lookout to the sea,
With her proud banner over me:
But from my lips thanksgiving broke,
As God in battle thunder spoke,

And that Black Idol, breeding drouth
And dearth of human sympathy
Throughout the sweet and sensuous South,
    Was, with its chains and human yoke,
Blown hellward from the cannon's mouth,
    While Freedom cheered behind the smoke!

SOLDIERS

Neither is money the sinews of war (as it is trivially said).
—Francis Bacon, *Of the Greatness of Kingdoms*

The Civil War was America's bloodiest conflict, with casualties on both sides exceeding the total dead of all other wars in United States history, including the two World Wars.[1] The terrible slaughter took its grim toll. After two years of fighting in battles where strategic decisions were often heavily influenced by the reported numbers of the opposition, additional recruits became critical. Neither side could expect to depend on volunteers—or to win the war, given the terrible attrition to their forces. Both the Union and the Confederacy passed legislation to initiate and enforce conscription; these became the first drafts in U.S. history.

At the beginning of the war, when each side anticipated swift and relatively painless victory, the volunteer armies were filled with the fire and dreams of glory that had led them to fight for the right to live by their differing principles. The first poems in this section speak of the early promise and bravery of the Blue and the Gray; the later poems move on to a grimmer reality.

Walt Whitman's "Bivouac on a Mountainside" is a glorious vision of a night encampment, tempered only by an image of the stars, "far, far out of reach, studded, breaking out, the eternal stars." "An Army Corps on the March" paints a vivid portrait of the Northern troops in action, while in "The Bivouac in the Snow," Margaret Junkin Preston leaves behind the romance of war in a somber poem that champions the bravery of the Southern soldier. Preston may well have

1. The source for battle statistics given is James M. McPherson, *Battle Cry of Freedom,* xix.

seen action in the field; she was married to Professor J. T. L. Preston, founder of the Virginia Military Institute.

When he wrote "Running the Batteries" in 1863, Herman Melville's hard-won literary reputation was already beginning to wane and it was not until his "rediscovery" in the 1920s that he received lasting kudos as one of America's greatest novelists. His narrative poem is the tale of Ulysses S. Grant's hard-won capture of Vicksburg in 1863, which proved to be one of the North's critical strategic victories.

The Civil War was the last war to use cavalry troops, and even then the invention of new and more efficient weapons had already begun to alter forever the strategy and practice of war. "Cavalry Crossing a Ford" is typical Whitman, and he presents a clear, strong portrait of the subject. "Roll-Call" by Nathaniel Graham Shepherd addresses the darker side of glory, bearing witness to the terrible losses suffered by the soldiers of both sides—the soldiers who were in fact the bloody sinews of the Civil War.

BIVOUAC ON A MOUNTAINSIDE
Walt Whitman

★ ★ ★ ★ ★ ★ ★

I see before me now a traveling army halting,
Below, a fertile valley spread, with barns and the orchards
    of summer,
Behind, the terraced sides of a mountain, abrupt, in places rising
    high,
Broken, with rocks, with clinging cedars, with tall shapes dingily
    seen,
The numerous camp-fires scattered near and far, some away up on
    the mountain,
The shadowy forms of men and horses, looming, large-sized,
    flickering,
And over all the sky—the sky! far, far out of reach, studded,
    breaking out, the eternal stars.

AN ARMY CORPS ON THE MARCH
Walt Whitman

★ ★ ★ ★ ★ ★ ★

With its cloud of skirmishers in advance,
With now the sound of a single shot snapping
    like a whip, and now an irregular volley,
The swarming ranks press on and on, the
    dense brigades press on,
Glittering dimly, toiling under the sun—the
    dust-cover'd men,
In columns rise and fall to the undulations
    of the ground,
With artillery interspers'd—the wheels rumble,
    the horses sweat,
As the army corps advances.

THE BIVOUAC IN THE SNOW
Margaret Junkin Preston (1820–1897)

Halt!—the march is over,
  Day is almost done;
Loose the cumbrous knapsack,
  Drop the heavy gun.
Chilled and wet and weary,
  Wander to and fro,
Seeking wood to kindle
  Fires amidst the snow.

Round the bright blaze gather,
  Heed not sleet nor cold;
Ye are Spartan soldiers,
  Stout and brave and bold.
Never Xerxian army
  Yet subdued a foe
Who but asked a blanket
  On a bed of snow.

Shivering, 'midst the darkness,
  Christian men are found,
There devoutly kneeling
  On the frozen ground—
Pleading for their country,
  In its hour of woe—
For its soldiers marching
  Shoeless through the snow.

Lost in heavy slumbers,
    Free from toil and strife,
Dreaming of their dear ones—
    Home, and child, and wife—
Tentless they are lying,
    While the fires burn low—
Lying in their blankets,
    'Midst December's snow.

RUNNING THE BATTERIES
Herman Melville (1819–1891)

* * * * * * *

As observed from the anchorage above Vicksburg, April, 1863

A moonless night—a friendly one;
  A haze dimmed the shadowy shore
As the first lampless boat slid silent on;
  Hist! and we spake no more;
We but pointed, and stilly, to what we saw.

We felt the dew, and seemed to feel
  The secret like a burden laid.
The first boat melts; and a second keel
  Is blent with the foliaged shade—
Their midnight rounds have the rebel officers made?

Unspied as yet. A third—a fourth—
  Gunboat and transport in Indian file
Upon the war-path, smooth from the North;
  But the watch may they hope to beguile?
The manned river-batteries stretch far mile on mile.

A flame leaps out; they are seen;
  Another and another gun roars;
We tell the course of the boats through the screen
  By each further fort that pours,
And we guess how they jump from their beds on
    those shrouded shores.

Converging fires. We speak, though low:
   "That blastful furnace can they thread?"
"Why, Shadrach, Meshach, and Abednego
   Came out all right, we read;
The Lord, be sure, he helps his people, Ned."

How we strain our gaze. On bluffs they shun
   A golden growing flame appears—
Confirms to a silvery steadfast one:
   "The town is afire!" crows Hugh; "three cheers!"
Lot stops his mouth: "Nay, lad, better three tears."

A purposed light; it shows our fleet;
   Yet a little late in its searching ray,
So far and strong that in phantom cheat
   Lank on the deck our shadows lay;
The shining flag-ship stings their guns to furious play.

How dread to mark her near the glare
   And glade of death the beacon throws
Athwart the racing waters there;
   One by one each plainer grows,
Then speeds a blazoned target to our gladdened foes.

The impartial cresset lights as well
   The fixed forts to the boats that run;
And, plunged from the ports, their answers swell
   Back to each fortress dun;
Ponderous words speaks every monster gun.

Fearless they flash through gates of flame,
   The salamanders hard to hit,
Though vivid shows each bulky frame;
   And never the batteries intermit,
Nor the boat's huge guns; they fire and flit.

Anon a lull. The beacon dies.
  "Are they out of that strait accurst?"
But other flames now dawning rise,
  Not mellowly brilliant like the first,
But rolled in smoke, whose whitish volumes burst.

A baleful brand, a hurrying torch
  Whereby anew the boats are seen—
A burning transport all alurch!
  Breathless we gaze; yet still we glean
Glimpses of beauty as we eager lean.

The effulgence takes an amber glow
  Which bathes the hillside villas far;
Affrighted ladies mark the show
  Painting the pale magnolia—
The fair, false, Circe light of cruel War.

The barge drifts doomed, a plague-struck one,
  Shoreward in yawls the sailors fly.
But the gauntlet now is nearly run,
  The spleenful forts by fits reply,
And the burning boat dies down in morning's sky.

All out of range. Adieu, Messieurs!
  Jeers, as it speeds, our parting gun.
So burst we through their barriers
  And menaces every one;
So Porter proves himself a brave man's son.

CAVALRY CROSSING A FORD

Walt Whitman

★ ★ ★ ★ ★ ★ ★

Behold the silvery river, in it the splashing horses loitering
    stop to drink,
Behold the brown-faced men, each group, each person, a picture,
    the negligent rest on the saddles,
Some emerge on the opposite bank, others are just entering
    the ford—while,
Scarlet and blue and snowy white,
The guidon flags flutter gayly in the wind.

ROLL-CALL

Nathaniel Graham Shepherd (1834–1888)

★ ★ ★ ★ ★ ★ ★

"Corporal Green!" the Orderly cried;
  "Here!" was the answer loud and clear,
  From the lips of a soldier who stood near,—
And "Here!" was the word the next replied.

"Cyrus Drew!"—then a silence fell;
  This time no answer followed the call;
  Only his rear-man had seen him fall:
Killed or wounded—he could not tell.

There they stood in the failing light,
  These men of battle, with grave, dark looks,
  As plain to be read as open books,
While slowly gathered the shades of night.

The fern on the hillsides was splashed with blood,
  And down in the corn, where the poppies grew,
  Were redder stains than the poppies knew,
And crimson-dyed was the river's flood.

For the foe had crossed from the other side,
  That day, in the face of a murderous fire
  That swept them down in its terrible ire;
And their life-blood went to color the tide.

"Herbert Cline!"—At the call there came
　　Two stalwart soldiers into the line,
　　Bearing between them this Herbert Cline,
Wounded and bleeding, to answer his name.

"Ezra Kerr!"—and a voice answered "Here!"
　　"Hiram Kerr!"—but no man replied.
　　They were brothers, these two; the sad wind sighed,
And a shudder crept through the cornfield near.

"Ephraim Deane!"—then a soldier spoke:
　　"Deane carried our regiment's colors," he said,
　　"When our ensign was shot; I left him dead,
Just after the enemy wavered and broke.

"Close to the roadside his body lies;
　　I paused a moment and gave him to drink;
　　He murmured his mother's name, I think,
And Death came with it and closed his eyes."

'Twas a victory, yes; but it cost us dear:
　　For that company's roll, when called at night,
　　Of a hundred men who went into the fight,
Numbered but twenty that answered *"Here!"*

DEEDS
OF
VALOR

Legends are the only guaranteed survivors of any war, and the Civil War's real and folk heroes still live on in both northern and southern history. Many of these heroes are remembered in the eloquent poetry of the period.

Edmund Clarence Stedman, a Connecticut-born banker and poet and a war correspondent during the Civil War, found his inspiration for "Kearny at Seven Pines" in a newspaper account of a ringing retort made by Brigadier-General Philip Kearny to a colonel at the battle of Seven Pines in June 1862. The dramatic Union victory and dreadful death toll at Chancellorsville is the subject of George Parsons Lathrop's epic "Keenan's Charge." Lathrop, who was born in Hawaii, was married to Nathaniel Hawthorne's daughter, Rose, and made his literary career by editing and adapting editions of Hawthorne's works.

Francis Orray Ticknor, the author of "Little Giffen," was a physician who literally saved sixteen-year-old Isaac Newton Giffen of Tennessee from death's door in October 1864. Giffen was subsequently killed in one of the closing battles of the war, but the boy soldier has been truly immortalized with this poem. Clinton Scollard's "The Daughter of the Regiment" is a stirring tribute to Kady Brownell's heroism during the Fifth Rhode Island Regiment's battle for New Berne and Roanoke Island on March 14, 1862.

In "Sheridan's Ride," Thomas Buchanan Read depicts the valor of General Philip H. Sheridan during one of the most successful deployments of Union cavalry in the Valley of Virginia in 1864. This poem, the most famous work of a minor Pennsylvania portrait painter and poet, contributes greatly to the mythology both of Sheridan and of his brave horse. "The General's Death" by Joseph O'Connor commemorates General George W. Taylor, who died at the Second Bull Run on August 27, 1862.

Finally, with "The Volunteer," Elbridge Jefferson Cutler honored not just one but all of the brave men of the 74th New York Infantry. This valiant Civil War volunteer is the unknown soldier who goes, as Cutler wrote: " 'where the bugles call,' he said, 'and rifles glean, I follow, though I die!' "

KEARNY AT SEVEN PINES
Edmund Clarence Stedman (1833–1908)

★ ★ ★ ★ ★ ★ ★

So that soldierly legend is still on its journey,—
  That story of Kearny who knew not to yield!
'Twas the day when with Jameson, fierce Berry, and Birney,
  Against twenty thousand he rallied the field.
Where the red volleys poured, where the clamor rose highest,
  Where the dead lay in clumps through the dwarf oak and pine,
Where the aim from the thicket was surest and nighest,—
  No charge like Phil Kearny's along the whole line.

When the battle went ill, and the bravest were solemn,
  Near the dark Seven Pines, where we still held our ground,
He rode down the length of the withering column,
  And his heart at our war-cry leapt up with a bound;
He snuffed, like his charger, the wind of the powder,—
  His sword waved us on and we answered the sign;
Loud our cheer as we rushed, but his laugh rang the louder.
  "There's the devil's own fun, boys, along the whole line!"

How he strode his brown steed! How we saw his blade brighten
  In the one hand still left,—and the reins in his teeth!
He laughed like a boy when the holidays heighten,
  But a soldier's glance shot from his visor beneath.
Up came the reserves to the mellay infernal,
  Asking where to go in,—through the clearing or pine?
"O, anywhere! Forward! 'Tis all the same, Colonel:
  You'll find lovely fighting along the whole line!"

Oh, evil the black shroud of night at Chantilly,
  That hid him from sight of his brave men and tried!
Foul, foul sped the bullet that clipped the white lily,
  The flower of our knighthood, the whole army's pride!
Yet we dream that he still,—in that shadowy region
  Where the dead form their ranks at the wan drummer's sign,—
Rides on, as of old, down the length of his legion,
  And the word still is "Forward!" along the whole line.

KEENAN'S CHARGE

George Parsons Lathrop (1851–1898)

★ ★ ★ ★ ★ ★ ★

The sun had set;
The leaves with dew were wet:
Down fell a bloody dusk
On the woods, that second of May,
Where Stonewall's corps, like a beast of prey,
Tore through with angry tusk.

"They've trapped us, boys!"
Rose from our flank a voice.
With a rush of steel and smoke
On came the rebels straight,
Eager as love and wild as hate;
And our line reeled and broke;

Broke and fled.
Not one stayed—but the dead!
With curses, shrieks, and cries,
Horses and wagons and men
Tumbled back through the shuddering glen,
And above us the fading skies.

There's one hope, still—
Those batteries parked on the hill!
"Battery, wheel!" ('mid the roar)
"Pass pieces; fix prolonge to fire

Retiring. Trot!" In the panic dire
A bugle rings "Trot!"—and no more.

The horses plunged,
The cannon lurched and lunged,
To join the hopeless rout.
But suddenly rode a form
Calmly in front of the human storm,
With a stern, commanding shout:

"Align those guns!"
(We knew it was Pleasonton's.)
The cannoneers bent to obey,
And worked with a will at his word:
And the black guns moved as if *they* had heard.
But, ah, the dread delay!

"To wait is crime;
O God, for ten minutes' time!"
The General looked around.
There Keenan sat, like a stone,
With his three hundred horse alone,
Less shaken than the ground.

"Major, your men?"
"Are soldiers, General." "Then
Charge, Major! Do your best;
Hold the enemy back at all cost,
Till my guns are placed;—else the army is lost.
You die to save the rest!"

By the shrouded gleam of the western skies,
Brave Keenan looked into Pleasonton's eyes
For an instant—clear, and cool, and still;
Then, with a smile, he said: "I will."

"Cavalry, charge!" Not a man of them shrank.
Their sharp, full cheer, from rank to rank,
Rose joyously, with a willing breath—
Rose like a greeting hail to death.

Then forward they sprang, and spurred, and clashed;
Shouted the officers, crimson-sashed;
Rode well the men, each brave as his fellow,
In their faded coats of the blue and yellow;
And above in the air, with an instinct true,
Like a bird of war their pennon flew.

With clank of scabbards and thunder of steeds
And blades that shine like sunlit reeds,
And strong brown faces bravely pale
For fear their proud attempt shall fail,
Three hundred Pennsylvanians close
On twice ten thousand gallant foes.

Line after line the troopers came
To the edge of the wood that was ring'd with flame;
Rode in, and sabred, and shot—and fell;
Nor came one back his wounds to tell.
And full in the midst rose Keenan tall
In the gloom, like a martyr awaiting his fall,
While the circle-stroke of his sabre, swung
'Round his head, like a halo there, luminous hung.

Line after line—aye, whole platoons,
Struck dead in their saddles, of brave dragoons
By the maddened horses were onward borne
And into the vortex flung, trampled and torn;
As Keenan fought with his men, side by side.
So they rode, till there were no more to ride.

But over them, lying there shattered and mute,
What deep echo rolls?—'Tis a death-salute
From the cannon in place; for, heroes, you braved
Your fate not in vain; the army was saved!

Over them now—year following year—
Over their graves the pine-cones fall,
And the whippoorwill chants his spectre-call;
But they stir not again: they raise no cheer:

They have ceased. But their glory shall never cease,
Nor their light be quenched in the light of peace.
The rush of their charge is resounding still
That saved the army at Chancellorsville.

LITTLE GIFFEN
Francis Orray Ticknor (1822–1874)

★ ★ ★ ★ ★ ★ ★

Out of the focal and foremost fire,
Out of the hospital walls as dire,
Smitten of grape-shot and gangrene,
(Eighteenth battle, and *he* sixteen!)
Spectre! such as you seldom see,
Little Giffen, of Tennessee.

"Take him—and welcome!" the surgeons said;
"Little the doctor can help the dead!"
So we took him and brought him where
The balm was sweet in the summer air;
And we laid him down on a wholesome bed—
Utter Lazarus, heel to head!

And we watched the war with abated breath—
Skeleton boy against skeleton death.
Months of torture, how many such!
Weary weeks of the stick and crutch;
And still a glint of the steel-blue eye
Told of a spirit that wouldn't die.

And didn't. Nay, more! in death's despite
The crippled skeleton learned to write.
"Dear Mother," at first, of course; and then
"Dear Captain," inquiring about the men.
Captain's answer: "Of eighty-and-five,
Giffen and I are left alive."

Word of gloom from the war, one day;
"Johnston pressed at the front, they say."
Little Giffen was up and away;
A tear—his first—as he bade good-by,
Dimmed the glint of his steel-blue eye.
"I'll write, if spared!" There was news of the fight;
But none of Giffen. He did not write.

I sometimes fancy that, were I king
Of the princely knights of the Golden Ring,
With the song of the minstrel in mine ear,
And the tender legend that trembles here,
I'd give the best on his bended knee,
The whitest soul of my chivalry,
For Little Giffen, of Tennessee.

THE DAUGHTER OF
THE REGIMENT

Clinton Scollard (1860–1932)

★ ★ ★ ★ ★ ★ ★

Who with the soldiers was stanch danger-sharer,—
   Marched in the ranks through the shriek of the shell?
Who was their comrade, their brave color-bearer?
   Who but the resolute Kady Brownell!

Over the marshland and over the highland,
   Where'er the columns wound, meadow or dell,
Fared she, this daughter of little Rhode Island,—
   She, the intrepid one, Kady Brownell!

While the mad rout at Manassas was surging,
   When those around her fled wildly, or fell,
And the bold Beauregard onward was urging,
   Who so undaunted as Kady Brownell!

When gallant Burnside made dash upon Newberne,
   Sailing the Neuse 'gainst the sweep of the swell,
Watching the flag on the heaven's broad blue burn,
   Who higher hearted than Kady Brownell?

In the deep slough of the springtide debarking,
   Toiling o'er leagues that are weary to tell,
Time with the sturdiest soldiery marking,
   Forward, straight forward, strode Kady Brownell.

Reaching the lines where the army was forming,
  Forming to charge on those ramparts of hell,
When from the wood came her regiment swarming,
  What did she see there—this Kady Brownell?

See! why she saw that their friends thought them foemen;
  Muskets were levelled, and cannon as well!
Save them from direful destruction would no men?
  Nay, but this woman would,—Kady Brownell!

Waving her banner she raced for the clearing;
  Fronted them all, with her flag as a spell;
Ah, what a volley—a volley of cheering—
  Greeted the heroine, Kady Brownell!

Gone (and thank God!) are those red days of slaughter!
  Brethren again we in amity dwell;
Just one more cheer for the Regiment's Daughter!—
  Just one more cheer for her, Kady Brownell!

SHERIDAN'S RIDE
Thomas Buchanan Read (1822–1872)

★ ★ ★ ★ ★ ★

Up from the South, at break of day,
Bringing to Winchester fresh dismay,
The affrighted air with a shudder bore,
Like a herald in haste to the chieftain's door,
The terrible grumble, and rumble, and roar,
Telling the battle was on once more,
    And Sheridan twenty miles away.

And wider still those billows of war
Thundered along the horizon's bar;
And louder yet into Winchester rolled
The roar of that red sea uncontrolled,
Making the blood of the listener cold,
As he thought of the stake in that fiery fray,
    With Sheridan twenty miles away.

But there is a road from Winchester town,
A good, broad highway leading down:
And there, through the flush of the morning light,
A steed as black as the steeds of night
Was seen to pass, as with eagle flight;
As if he knew the terrible need,
He stretched away with his utmost speed.
Hills rose and fell, but his heart was gay,
    With Sheridan fifteen miles away.

Still sprang from those swift hoofs, thundering south,
The dust like smoke from the cannon's mouth,
Or the trail of a comet, sweeping faster and faster,
Foreboding to traitors the doom of disaster.
The heart of the steed and the heart of the master
Were beating like prisoners assaulting their walls,
Impatient to be where the battle-field calls;
Every nerve of the charger was strained to full play,
     With Sheridan only ten miles away.

Under his spurning feet, the road
Like an arrowy Alpine river flowed,
And the landscape sped away behind
Like an ocean flying before the wind;
And the steed, like a barque fed with furnace ire,
Swept on, with his wild eye full of fire;
But, lo! he is nearing his heart's desire;
He is snuffing the smoke of the roaring fray,
     With Sheridan only five miles away.

The first that the general saw were the groups
Of stragglers, and then the retreating troops;
What was done? what to do?—a glance told him both.
Then striking his spurs with a terrible oath,
He dashed down the line, 'mid a storm of huzzas,
And the wave of retreat checked its course there, because
The sight of the master compelled it to pause.
With foam and with dust the black charger was gray;
By the flash of his eye, and his red nostril's play,
He seemed to the whole great army to say:
"I have brought you Sheridan all the way
     From Winchester down to save the day."

Hurrah! hurrah for Sheridan!
Hurrah! hurrah for horse and man!

And when their statues are placed on high
Under the dome of the Union sky,
The American soldier's Temple of Fame,
There, with the glorious general's name,
Be it said, in letters both bold and bright:
"Here is the steed that saved the day
By carrying Sheridan into the fight,
From Winchester—twenty miles away!"

THE GENERAL'S DEATH
Joseph O'Connor (dates unknown)

★ ★ ★ ★ ★ ★ ★

The general dashed along the road
  Amid the pelting rain;
How joyously his bold face glowed
  To hear our cheers' refrain!

His blue blouse flapped in wind and wet,
  His boots were splashed with mire,
But round his lips a smile was set,
  And in his eyes a fire.

A laughing word, a gesture kind,—
  We did not ask for more,
With thirty weary miles behind,
  A weary fight before.

The gun grew light to every man,
  The crossed belts ceased their stress,
As onward to the column's van
  We watched our leader press.

Within an hour we saw him lie,
  A bullet in his brain,
His manly face turned to the sky,
  And beaten by the rain.

THE VOLUNTEER

Elbridge Jefferson Cutler (1831–1870)

★ ★ ★ ★ ★ ★ ★

"At dawn," he said, "I bid them all farewell,
    To go where bugles call and rifles gleam."
And with the restless thought asleep he fell,
    And glided into dream.

A great hot plain from sea to mountain spread,—
    Through it a level river slowly drawn:
He moved with a vast crowd, and at its head
    Streamed banners like the dawn.

There came a blinding flash, a deafening roar,
    And dissonant cries of triumph and dismay;
Blood trickled down the river's reedy shore,
    And with the dead he lay.

The morn broke in upon his solemn dream,
    And still, with steady pulse and deepening eye,
"Where bugles call," he said, "and rifles gleam,
    I follow, though I die!"

ENEMIES
AND
FRIENDS

The war that divided North and South and turned friends into enemies knew no distinctions in casualties. Officers who had once roomed together at West Point found themselves commanding opposing forces, but it was in the aftermath of battle that many men rediscovered their common bonds.

Francis Bret Harte, humorist and natural storyteller, was born in Albany, New York. He had a variety of careers, from digger in the California gold rush and editor-in-chief of the *Weekly Californian* to secretary of the United States Mint in San Francisco, editor of the *Overland Monthly,* and various consular appointments abroad. It was during his tenure at the Mint from 1864 to 1867 that he wrote most of his Civil War poetry, along with the humorous verse that brought him recognition in the East and the West. "The Aged Stranger" is Harte in his most ebullient and humorous mode.

Benjamin Sledd's poem, "United," speaks of the grim brotherhood of the battlefield, while John Reuben Thompson's "Music in Camp" expresses the power that music had—in camp and on the battlefield—to move memory and emotion. The setting of this poem is after the battle of Chancellorsville in May of 1863, when for several weeks the opposing forces remained encamped on opposite banks of the Rappahannock River, until Lee's invasion of the North ended in the battle of Gettysburg.

Frank H. Gassaway's moving work, "The Pride of Battery B," is set at the close of the first day's battle at Antietam, or Sharpsburg, on September 16, 1862. "Civil War" by Charles Dawson Shanly is often anthologized under the alternative title "The Fancy Shot." The poem first appeared in London's *Once a Week* as "Civile Bellum" and was dated "From the Once United States." This tale of a family torn and destroyed by war, in which a captain discovers that he has given a rifleman the order to shoot his own brother, is an infamous example of just what was possible in a nation divided.

THE AGED STRANGER
Francis Bret Harte (1836–1902)

★ ★ ★ ★ ★ ★

"I was with Grant"—the stranger said;
  Said the farmer, "Say no more,
But rest thee here at my cottage porch,
  For thy feet are weary and sore."

"I was with Grant"—the stranger said;
  Said the farmer, "Nay, no more,—
I prithee sit at my frugal board,
  And eat of my humble store.

"How fares my boy,—my soldier boy,
  Of the old Ninth Army Corps?
I warrant he bore him gallantly
  In the smoke and battle's roar!"

"I know him not," said the aged man,
  "And, as I remarked before,
I was with Grant"—"Nay, nay, I know,"
  Said the farmer, "say no more:

"He fell in battle,—I see, alas!
  Thou 'dst smooth these tidings o'er,—
Nay, speak the truth, whatever it be,
  Though it rend my bosom's core.

"How fell he,—with his face to the foe,
    Upholding the flag he bore?
Oh, say not that my boy disgraced
    The uniform that he wore!"

"I cannot tell," said the aged man,
    "And should have remarked before,
That I was with Grant,—in Illinois,—
    Some three years before the war."

Then the farmer spake him never a word,
    But beat with his fist full sore
That aged man, who had worked for Grant
    Some three years before the war.

UNITED
Benjamin Sledd (dates unknown)

★ ★ ★ ★ ★ ★ ★

All day it shook the land—grim battle's thunder tread;
And fields at morning green, at eve are trampled red.
But now, on the stricken scene, twilight and quiet fall;
Only, from hill to hill, night's tremulous voices call;
And comes from far along, where campfires warning burn,
The dread, hushed sound which tells of morning's sad return.

Timidly nature awakens; the stars come out overhead,
And a flood of moonlight breaks like a voiceless prayer
   for the dead.
And steals the blessed wind, like Odin's fairest daughter,
In viewless ministry, over the fields of slaughter;
Soothing the smitten life, easing the pang of death,
And bearing away on high the passing warrior's breath.

Two youthful forms are lying apart from the thickest fray,
The one in Northern blue, the other in Southern gray.
Around his lifeless foeman the arms of each are pressed,
And the head of one is pillowed upon the other's breast.
As if two loving brothers, wearied with work and play,
Had fallen asleep together, at close of the summer day.
Foeman were they, and brothers?—Again the battle's din,
With its sullen, cruel answer, from far away breaks in.

MUSIC IN CAMP

John Reuben Thompson (1823–1873)

★ ★ ★ ★ ★ ★ ★

Two armies covered hill and plain,
  Where Rappahannock's waters
Ran deeply crimsoned with the stain
  Of battle's recent slaughters.

The summer clouds lay pitched like tents
  In meads of heavenly azure;
And each dread gun of the elements
  Slept in its hid embrasure.

The breeze so softly blew it made
  No forest leaf to quiver,
And the smoke of the random cannonade
  Rolled slowly from the river.

And now, where circling hills looked down
  With cannon grimly planted,
O'er listless camp and silent town
  The golden sunset slanted.

When on the fervid air there came
  A strain—now rich, now tender;
The music seemed itself aflame
  With day's departing splendor.

A Federal band, which, eve and morn,
    Played measures brave and nimble,
Had just struck up, with flute and horn
    And lively clash of cymbal.

Down flocked the soldiers to the banks,
    Till, margined with its pebbles,
One wooded shore was blue with "Yanks,"
    And one was gray with "Rebels."

Then all was still, and then the band,
    With movement light and tricksy,
Made stream and forest, hill and strand,
    Reverberate with "Dixie."

The conscious stream with burnished glow
    Went proudly o'er its pebbles,
But thrilled throughout its deepest flow
    With yelling of the Rebels.

Again a pause, and then again
    The trumpets pealed sonorous,
And "Yankee Doodle" was the strain
    To which the shore gave chorus.

The laughing ripple shoreward flew,
    To kiss the shining pebbles;
Loud shrieked the swarming Boys in Blue
    Defiance to the Rebels.

And yet once more the bugles sang
    Above the stormy riot;
No shout upon the evening rang—
    There reigned a holy quiet.

The sad, slow stream its noiseless flood
   Poured o'er the glistening pebbles;
All silent now the Yankees stood,
   And silent stood the Rebels.

No unresponsive soul had heard
   That plaintive note's appealing,
So deeply "Home, Sweet Home" had stirred
   The hidden founts of feeling.

Or Blue or Gray, the soldier sees,
   As by the wand of fairy,
The cottage 'neath the live-oak trees,
   The cabin by the prairie.

Or cold or warm his native skies
   Bend in their beauty o'er him;
Seen through the tear-mist in his eyes,
   His loved ones stand before him.

As fades the iris after rain
   In April's tearful weather,
The vision vanished, as the strain
   And daylight died together.

But memory, waked by music's art,
   Expressed in simplest numbers,
Subdued the sternest Yankee's heart,
   Made light the Rebel's slumbers.

And fair the form of music shines,
   That bright, celestial creature,
Who still, 'mid war's embattled lines,
   Gave this one touch of Nature.

THE PRIDE OF BATTERY B

Frank H. Gassaway (dates unknown)

★ ★ ★ ★ ★ ★ ★

South Mountain towered on our right,
　　Far off the river lay,
And over on the wooded height
　　We held their lines at bay.

At last the mutt'ring guns were stilled,
　　The day died slow and wan.
At last their pipes the gunners filled,
　　The Sergeant's yarns began.

When,—as the wind a moment blew
　　Aside the fragrant flood
Our brierwoods raised,—within our view
　　A little maiden stood.

A tiny tot of six or seven;
　　From fireside fresh she seemed.
(Of such a little one in heaven
　　One soldier often dreamed.)

And as we started, her little hand
　　Went to her curly head
In grave salute; "And who are you?"
　　At length the Sergeant said.

54

"And where's your home?" he growled again.
    She lisped out, "Who is me?
Why, don't you know? I'm little Jane,
    The pride of Battery B.

"My home? Why, that was burned away,
    And pa and ma are dead,
And so I ride the guns all day
    Along with Sergeant Ned.

"And I've a drum that's not a toy,
    A cap with feathers too,
And I march beside the drummer-boy
    On Sundays at review.

"But now our bacca's all give out,
    The men can't have their smoke,
And so they're cross,—why, even Ned
    Won't play with me and joke.

"And the big Colonel said to-day—
    I hate to hear him swear—
He'd give a leg for a good pipe
    Like the Yanks have over there.

"And so I thought, when beat the drum,
    And the big guns were still,
I'd creep beneath the tent and come
    Out here across the hill.

"And beg, good Mister Yankee men,
    You'd give me some Lone Jack.
Please do—when we get some again
    I'll surely bring it back.

"Indeed I will, for Ned, says he,
　　If I do what I say
I'll be a general yet, maybe,
　　And ride a prancing bay."

We brimmed her tiny apron o'er;
　　You should have heard her laugh
As each man from his scanty store
　　Shook out a generous half.

To kiss that little mouth stooped down
　　A score of grimy men,
Until the Sergeant's husky voice
　　Said " 'Tention, squad!"—and then

We gave her escort, till good-night
　　The pretty waif we bid,
And watched her toddle out of sight—
　　Or else 'twas tears that hid

Her tiny form—nor turned about
　　A man, nor spoke a word,
Till after while a far, hoarse shout
　　Upon the wind we heard.

We sent it back, then cast sad eye
　　Upon the scene around.
A baby's hand had touched the tie
　　That brothers once had bound.

That's all—save when the dawn awoke
　　Again the work of hell,
And through the sullen clouds of smoke
　　The screaming missiles fell,

Our Gen'ral often rubbed his glass,
  And marvelled much to see
Not a single shell that whole day fell
  In the camp of Battery B.

CIVIL WAR
Charles Dawson Shanly (1811–1875)

★ ★ ★ ★ ★ ★ ★ ★

"Rifleman, shoot me a fancy shot
  Straight at the heart of yon prowling vidette;
Ring me a ball in the glittering spot
  That shines on his breast like an amulet!"

"Ah, captain! here goes for a fine-drawn bead,
  There's music around when my barrel's in tune!"
Crack! went the rifle, the messenger sped,
  And dead from his horse fell the ringing dragoon.

"Now, rifleman, steal through the bushes, and snatch
  From your victim some trinket to handsel first blood;
A button, a loop, or that luminous patch
  That gleams in the moon like a diamond stud!"

"O captain! I staggered, and sunk on my track,
  When I gazed on the face of that fallen vidette,
For he looked so like you, as he lay on his back,
  That my heart rose upon me, and masters me yet.

"But I snatched off the trinket,—this locket of gold;
  An inch from the centre my lead broke its way,
Scarce grazing the picture, so fair to behold,
  Of a beautiful lady in bridal array."

"Ha! rifleman, fling me the locket!—'tis she,
   My brother's young bride, and the fallen dragoon
Was her husband—Hush! soldier, 'twas Heaven's decree,
   We must bury him there, by the light of the moon!

"But hark! the far bugles their warnings unite;
   War is a virtue,—weakness a sin;
There's a lurking and loping around us to-night;
   Load again, rifleman, keep your hand in!"

FAMILY

The great tide of the war ebbed and flowed, reputations were won and lost with battles, heroic deeds and horrors done, and numerous lives laid down in the service of both the Union and the Confederacy. In or out of action, the men on both sides held tightly to the memories of their families—for inspiration, for consolation, and in hope of the end of the war.

"The Picket-Guard" by Ethel Lynn Beers is set in the autumn of 1861. In the relative calm along the Potomac following the First Battle of Bull Run, a sentry walks his route in the quiet darkness, thinking of his children asleep at home in the mountains, until a rifle blast from the bushes ends his dreaming forever.

Women of the North and South alike wished for their fighting men, if not fame and glory, at least a peaceful and honored grave. This is the theme of "A Message" by Elizabeth Stuart Phelps Ward.

In "Christmas Night of '62," Lee's bloody repulse of Burnside's attempt to drive on to Richmond was only thirteen days past, but the thoughts of poet William Gordon McCabe and his fellow soldiers in the Army of Northern Virginia are all turned toward family and home. McCabe's other poem, "Dreaming in the Trenches," is about the Petersburg, Virginia, trenches in 1864, and his vivid imagery of home records the solitude of the tented fields, where thousands of men from many sections were gathered, each alone with his own thoughts. Shortly afterward, Lee abandoned besieged Petersburg, and Richmond finally fell to the North in one of the concluding battles of the war.

The theme of the final poem in this section, Walt Whitman's "Come Up from the Fields, Father," concerns the family's thoughts of the soldier. In a scene that is forever to be repeated throughout history, Whitman's blunt verse sets the scene: "Lo, 'tis autumn"; opens the senses: "Smell you the smell of the grapes on the vines? Smell you the buckwheat where the bees were lately buzzing?"; and delivers the blow: the letter announcing the death of the only son in an Ohio farm family.

THE PICKET-GUARD

Ethel Lynn Beers (1827–1879)

★ ★ ★ ★ ★ ★ ★

"All quiet along the Potomac," they say,
  "Except now and then a stray picket
Is shot, as he walks on his beat to and fro,
  By a rifleman hid in the thicket.
'Tis nothing: a private or two now and then
  Will not count in the news of the battle;
Not an officer lost—only one of the men,
  Moaning out, all alone, the death-rattle."

All quiet along the Potomac to-night,
  Where the soldiers lie peacefully dreaming;
Their tents in the rays of the clear autumn moon,
  Or the light of the watch-fire, are gleaming.
A tremulous sigh of the gentle night-wind
  Through the forest leaves softly is creeping;
While the stars up above, with their glittering eyes,
  Keep guard, for the army is sleeping.

There's only the sound of the lone sentry's tread,
  As he tramps from the rock to the fountain,
And thinks of the two in the low trundle-bed
  Far away in the cot on the mountain.
His musket falls slack; his face, dark and grim,
  Grows gentle with memories tender,
As he mutters a prayer for the children asleep—
  For their mother—may Heaven defend her!

The moon seems to shine just as brightly as then,
That night, when the love yet unspoken
Leaped up to his lips—when low-murmured vows
Were pledged to be ever unbroken.
Then drawing his sleeve roughly over his eyes,
He dashes off tears that are welling,
And gathers his gun closer up to its place
As if to keep down the heart-swelling.

He passes the fountain, the blasted pine-tree;
The footstep is lagging and weary;
Yet onward he goes, through the broad belt of light,
Towards the shade of the forest so dreary.
Hark! was it the night-wind that rustled the leaves?
Was it moonlight so wondrously flashing?
It looked like a rifle . . . "Ha! Mary, good-by!"
The red life-blood is ebbing and plashing.

All quiet along the Potomac to-night—
No sound save the rush of the river,
While soft falls the dew on the face of the dead—
The picket's off duty forever!

A MESSAGE

Elizabeth Stuart Phelps Ward (1844–1911)

★ ★ ★ ★ ★ ★ ★

Was there ever message sweeter
   Than that one from Malvern Hill,
From a grim old fellow,—you remember?
   Dying in the dark at Malvern Hill.
With his rough face turned a little,
   On a heap of scarlet sand,
They found him, just within the thicket,
   With a picture in his hand,—

With a stained and crumpled picture
   Of a woman's aged face;
Yet there seemed to leap a wild entreaty,
   Young and living—tender—from the face
When they flashed the lantern on it,
   Gilding all the purple shade,
And stooped to raise him softly,—
   "That's my mother, sir," he said.

"Tell her"—but he wandered, slipping
   Into tangled words and cries,—
Something about Mac and Hooker,
   Something dropping through the cries
About the kitten by the fire,
   And mother's cranberry-pies; and there
The words fell, and an utter
   Silence brooded in the air.

Just as he was drifting from them,
    Out into the dark, alone
(Poor old mother, waiting for your message,
    Waiting with the kitten, all alone!),
Through the hush his voice broke,—"Tell her—
    Thank you, Doctor—when you can,—
Tell her that I kissed her picture,
    And wished I'd been a better man."

Ah, I wonder if the red feet
    Of departed battle-hours
May not leave for us their searching
    Message from those distant hours.
Sisters, daughters, mothers, think you,
    Would your heroes now or then,
Dying, kiss your pictured faces,
    Wishing they'd been better men?

CHRISTMAS NIGHT OF '62

William Gordon McCabe (1841–1920)

* * * * * * *

The wintry blast goes wailing by,
　　The snow is falling overhead;
　　I hear the lonely sentry's tread,
And distant watch-fires light the sky.

Dim forms go flitting through the gloom;
　　The soldiers cluster round the blaze
　　To talk of other Christmas days,
And softly speak of home and home.

My sabre swinging overhead
　　Gleams in the watch-fire's fitful glow,
　　While fiercely drives the blinding snow,
And memory leads me to the dead.

My thoughts go wandering to and fro,
　　Vibrating 'twixt the Now and Then;
　　I see the low-browed home again,
The old hall wreathed with mistletoe.

And sweetly from the far-off years
　　Comes borne the laughter faint and low,
　　The voices of the Long Ago!
My eyes are wet with tender tears.

I feel again the mother-kiss,
    I see again the glad surprise
    That lightened up the tranquil eyes
And brimmed them o'er with tears of bliss,

As, rushing from the old hall-door,
    She fondly clasped her wayward boy—
    Her face all radiant with the joy
She felt to see him home once more.

My sabre swinging on the bough
    Gleams in the watch-fire's fitful glow,
    While fiercely drives the blinding snow
Aslant upon my saddened brow.

Those cherished faces all are gone!
    Asleep within the quiet graves
    Where lies the snow in drifting waves,—
And I am sitting here alone.

There's not a comrade here to-night
    But knows that loved ones far away
    On bended knees this night will pray:
"God bring our darling from the fight."

But there are none to wish me back,
    For me no yearning prayers arise.
    The lips are mute and closed the eyes—
My home is in the bivouac.

DREAMING IN THE TRENCHES

William Gordon McCabe

I picture her there in the quaint old room,
　　Where the fading fire-light starts and falls,
Alone in the twilight's tender gloom
　　With the shadows that dance on the dim-lit walls.

Alone, while those faces look silently down
　　From their antique frames in a grim repose—
Slight scholarly Ralph in his Oxford gown,
　　And stanch Sir Alan, who died for Montrose.

There are gallants gay in crimson and gold,
　　There are smiling beauties with powdered hair,
But she sits there, fairer a thousand-fold,
　　Leaning dreamily back in her low arm-chair.

And the roseate shadows of fading light
　　Softly clear steal over the sweet young face,
Where a woman's tenderness blends to-night
　　With the guileless pride of a knightly race.

Her hands lie clasped in a listless way
　　On the old *Romance*—which she holds on her knee—
Of Tristram, the bravest of knights in the fray,
　　And Iseult, who waits by the sounding sea.

And her proud, dark eyes wear a softened look
  As she watches the dying embers fall:
Perhaps she dreams of the knight in the book,
  Perhaps of the pictures that smile on the wall.

What fancies I wonder are thronging her brain,
  For her cheeks flush warm with a crimson glow!
Perhaps—ah! me, how foolish and vain!
  But I'd give my life to believe it so!

Well, whether I ever march home again
  To offer my love and a stainless name,
Or whether I die at the head of my men,—
  I'll be true to the end all the same.

COME UP FROM THE FIELDS, FATHER
Walt Whitman

★ ★ ★ ★ ★ ★

Come up from the fields, father, here's a letter from our Pete,
And come to the front door, mother, here's
    a letter from thy dear son.

Lo, 'tis autumn,
Lo, where the trees, deeper green, yellower and redder,
Cool and sweeten Ohio's villages with leaves
    fluttering in the moderate wind,
Where apples ripe in the orchards hang and
    grapes on the trellis'd vines,
(Smell you the smell of the grapes on the vines?
Smell you the buckwheat where the bees were lately buzzing?)
Above all, lo, the sky so calm, so transparent
    after the rain, and with wondrous clouds,
Below too, all calm, all vital and beautiful,
    and the farm prospers well.

Down in the fields all prospers well,
But now from the fields come, father, come
    at the daughter's call,
And come to the entry, mother, to the front
    door come right away.

Fast as she can she hurries, something ominous,
    her steps trembling,
She does not tarry to smooth her hair nor
    adjust her cap.

Open the envelope quickly,
O this is not our son's writing, yet his name
    is sign'd,
O a strange hand writes for our dear son,
    O stricken mother's soul!
All swims before her eyes, flashes with black,
    she catches the main words only,
Sentences broken, *gunshot wound in the breast,*
    cavalry skirmish, taken to hospital,
At present low, but will soon be better.

Ah, now the single figure to me,
Amid all teeming and wealthy Ohio with all
    its cities and farms,
Sickly white in the face and dull in the head,
    very faint,
By the jamb of a door leans.

Grieve not so, dear mother (the just-grown
    daughter speaks through her sobs,
The little sisters huddle around speechless and
    dismay'd),
See, dearest mother, the letter says Pete will
    soon be better.

Alas, poor boy, he will never be better (nor maybe
    needs to be better, that brave and simple soul),
While they stand at home at the door he is
    dead already,
The only son is dead.

But the mother needs to be better,
She with thin form presently drest in black,
By day her meals untouch'd, then at night
    fitfully sleeping, often waking,
In the midnight waking, weeping, longing with
    one deep longing,
O that she might withdraw unnoticed, silent
    from life escape and withdraw,
To follow, to seek, to be with her dear dead
    son.

IN
MEMORIAM

"**G**lory and honor and fame and everlasting laudation . . ." Much of the poetry of commemoration from the Civil War suffers from magniloquence even beyond the traditional high-flown style of the period. The subjects of these poems, however, hold their places firmly in American history.

In April of 1862, the battle of Shiloh turned the Civil War from a "limited war" begun at Fort Sumter into total war. Twenty thousand men from both sides died at Shiloh, a number equal to all of the casualties from the previous battles combined.[2] Herman Melville's eloquent "Shiloh, A Requiem" remembers this battle.

"Pelham" by James Ryder Randall is a tribute to Confederate Major John Pelham, who died while commanding the Horse Artillery in the Battle of Kellysville on March 17, 1863. Randall, born in Baltimore, is best known for his famous battle cry "My Maryland" (included here in the "Famous Lyrics" section). John Reuben Thompson's "Ashby" celebrates Turner Ashby of Virginia, who distinguished himself as a cavalry leader under Stonewall Jackson in the Shenandoah Valley Campaign of May–June 1862.

"Stonewall" Jackson earned his remarkable name at the First Manassas on July 21, 1861, when his brigade halted a ferocious Union assault and turned the battle into a smashing Confederate victory. Jackson became one of the most successful and respected leaders of the Southern forces. It has been said that a Union soldier captured by Jackson's forces at Harper's Ferry remarked about Jackson, "Well, he's not much to look at, but if we'd only had *him,* we'd never have been in this fix." John Williamson Palmer wrote "Stonewall Jackson's Way" in Garret County, Maryland, on September 16, 1862, with the roar of the guns

[2]McPherson, *Battle Cry of Freedom,* 413.

still ringing in his ears. He added the final stanza to his poem on the following day, after the Confederate victory was a fact. Sidney Lanier's "The Dying Words of Stonewall Jackson" is an eloquent memorial to Jackson, who died on May 10, 1863, after falling on the battlefield at Chancellorsville. Lanier, a Georgia-born musician and writer, served with the Second Georgia Battalion of the Macon Volunteers through the Seven Days' Battles and was captured while running the blockades between Wilmington, North Carolina, and the Bermudas.

Kate Brownlee Sherwood's "Albert Sidney Johnson" commemorates that formidable Confederate General, who died in action at Shiloh in 1862. Johnson was worth more than an army of 10,000 men, or so said Confederate President Jefferson Davis. Sherwood was bipartisan in her verse, and her "Thomas at Chickamauga" pays homage to Union General George H. Thomas, known as "the rock of Chickamauga," who commanded the northern troops during the deadly battle of Chickamauga in September 1863.

William Tuckey Meredith, author of "Farragut," served under "Daring Dave" Farragut in the battle of Mobile Bay on August 5, 1864. Meredith later became the secretary of this Union Navy paragon, whose well-timed capture of New Orleans in 1862 proved a major strategic victory for the North. Richard Watson Gilder wrote "Sherman" following the death of General William Tecumseh Sherman in New York City on February 14, 1891. Gilder, who was born in Bordentown, New Jersey, participated in the defense of Carlisle, Pennsylvania, when Lee's northern invasion ended at Gettysburg. His literary career flourished after the war and he became editor-in-chief of *The Century* magazine in 1881.

Henry Abbey's "On a Great Warrior" is a dramatic elegy written in 1885, shortly after the death of Ulysses S. Grant, commander-in-chief of the Union Army and 18th President of the United States (1869–1877). Robert E. Lee, general-in-chief of the Confederate Armies, is honored in "Robert E. Lee" by Julia Ward Howe, best known for her "Battle-Hymn of the Republic" (included in the "Famous Lyrics" section). William Vaughn Moody, Indiana-born poet and playwright, composed his splendid "An Ode in Time of Hesitation" after he saw a statue of Robert Gould Shaw, who was killed while assaulting Fort Wagner, July 18, 1863, at the head of the first enlisted black regiment, the 54th Massachusetts.

SHILOH, A REQUIEM
Herman Melville

★ ★ ★ ★ ★ ★ ★

April, 1862

Skimming lightly, wheeling still,
  The swallows fly low

    Over the fields in clouded days,
      The forest-field of Shiloh—
    Over the field where April rain
    Solaced the parched one stretched in pain
    Through the pause of night
    That followed the Sunday fight
      Around the church of Shiloh—
    The church so lone, the log-built one,
    That echoed to many a parting groan
        And natural prayer
      Of dying foemen mingled there—
    Foemen at morn, but friends at eve—
      Fame or country least their care:
    (What like a bullet can undeceive!)
      But now they lie low,
    While over them the swallows skim,
      And all is hushed at Shiloh.

PELHAM

James Ryder Randall (1839–1908)

Just as the spring came laughing through the strife,
　　With all its gorgeous cheer,
In the bright April of historic life
　　Fell the great cannoneer.

The wondrous lulling of a hero's breath
　　His bleeding country weeps;
Hushed, in the alabaster arms of Death,
　　Our young Marcellus sleeps.

Nobler and grander than the child of Rome,
　　Curbing his chariot steeds,
The knightly scion of a Southern home
　　Dazzled the land with deeds.

Gentlest and bravest in the battle's brunt—
　　The Champion of the Truth—
He bore his banner in the very front
　　Of our immortal youth.

A clang of sabres 'mid Virginian snow,
　　The fiery pang of shells—
And there's a wail of immemorial woe
　　In Alabama dells.

The pennon droops that led the sacred band
  Along the crimson field;
The meteor blade sinks from the nerveless hand
  Over the spotless shield.

We gazed and gazed upon that beauteous face,
  While, round the lips and eyes,
Couched in their marble slumber, flashed the grace
  Of a divine surprise.

O mother of a blessed soul on high!
  Thy tears may soon be shed—
Think of thy boy with princes of the sky,
  Among the Southern dead.

How must he smile on this dull world beneath,
  Fevered with swift renown;
He, with the martyr's amaranthine wreath,
  Twining the victor's crown!

ASHBY

John Reuben Thompson

★ ★ ★ ★ ★ ★ ★

To the brave all homage render!
  Weep, ye skies of June!
With a radiance pure and tender,
  Shine, O saddened moon;
"Dead upon the field of glory!"—
Hero fit for song and story—
  Lies our bold dragoon.

Well they learned, whose hands have slain him,
  Braver, knightlier foe
Never fought 'gainst Moor or Paynim—
  Rode at Templestowe:
With a mien how high and joyous,
'Gainst the hordes that would destroy us,
  Went he forth, we know.

Nevermore, alas! shall sabre
  Gleam around his crest—
Fought his fight, fulfilled his labor,
  Stilled his manly breast—
All unheard sweet Nature's cadence,
  Trump of fame and voice of maidens,
  Now he takes his rest.

Earth, that all too soon hath bound him,
    Gently wrap his clay!
Linger lovingly around him,
    Light of dying day!
Softly fall, ye summer showers;
Birds and bees among the flowers
    Make the gloom seem gay!

There, throughout the coming ages—
    When his sword is rust,
And his deeds in classic pages—
    Mindful of her trust
Shall Virginia, bending lowly,
Still a ceaseless vigil holy
    Keep above his dust.

STONEWALL JACKSON'S WAY
John Williamson Palmer (1825–1906)

★ ★ ★ ★ ★ ★ ★

Come, stack arms, men! pile on the rails,
    Stir up the camp-fire bright;
No growling if the canteen fails,
    We'll make a roaring night.
Here Shenandoah brawls along,
There burly Blue Ridge echoes strong,
To swell the Brigade's rousing song
    Of "Stonewall Jackson's way."

We see him now—the queer slouched hat
    Cocked o'er his eye askew;
The shrewd, dry smile; the speech so pat,
    So calm, so blunt, so true.
The "Blue-light Elder" knows 'em well;
Says he, "That's Banks—he's fond of shell;
Lord save his soul! we'll give him—" well!
    That's "Stonewall Jackson's way."

Silence! ground arms! kneel all! caps off!
    Old Massa's goin' to pray.
Strangle the fool that dares to scoff!
    Attention! it's his way.
Appealing from his native sod
In forma pauperis to God:
"Lay bare Thine arm; stretch forth Thy rod!
    Amen!"—That's "Stonewall's way."

He's in the saddle now. Fall in!
　　Steady! the whole brigade!
Hill's at the ford, cut off; we'll win
　　His way out, ball and blade!
What matter if our shoes are worn?
What matter if our feet are torn?
"Quick step! we're with him before morn!"
　　That's "Stonewall Jackson's way."

The sun's bright lances rout the mists
　　Of morning, and, by George!
Here's Longstreet, struggling in the lists,
　　Hemmed in an ugly gorge.
Pope and his Dutchmen, whipped before;
"Bay'nets and grape!" hear Stonewall roar;
"Charge, Stuart! Pay off Ashby's score!"
　　In "Stonewall Jackson's way."

Ah, Maiden! wait and watch and yearn
　　For news of Stonewall's band.
Ah, Widow! read, with eyes that burn,
　　That ring upon thy hand.
Ah, Wife! sew on, pray on, hope on;
Thy life shall not be all forlorn;
The foe had better ne'er been born
　　That gets in "Stonewall's way."

THE DYING WORDS
OF STONEWALL JACKSON

Sidney Lanier (1842–1881)

★ ★ ★ ★ ★ ★ ★

"Order A. P. Hill to prepare for battle."
"Tell Major Hawks to advance the commissary train."
"Let us cross the river and rest in the shade."

The stars of Night contain the glittering Day
And rain his glory down with sweeter grace
Upon the dark World's grand, enchanted face—
    All loth to turn away.

And so the Day, about to yield his breath,
Utters the stars unto the listening Night,
To stand for burning fare-thee-wells of light
    Said on the verge of death.

O hero-life that lit us like the sun!
O hero-words that glittered like the stars
And stood and shone above the gloomy wars
    When the hero-life was done!

The phantoms of a battle came to dwell
I' the fitful vision of his dying eyes—
Yet even in battle-dreams, he sends supplies
    To those he loved so well.

His army stands in battle-line arrayed:
His couriers fly: all's done: now God decide!
—And not till then saw he the Other Side
    Or would accept the shade.

Thou land whose sun is gone, thy stars remain!
Still shine the words that miniature his deeds.
O thrice-beloved, where'er thy great heart bleeds,
    Solace hast thou for pain!

ALBERT SIDNEY JOHNSTON

Kate Brownlee Sherwood (1841–1914)

I hear again the tread of war go thundering through the land,
And Puritan and Cavalier are clinching neck and hand,
Round Shiloh church the furious foes have met to thrust and slay,
Where erst the peaceful sons of Christ were wont to kneel and
     pray.

The wrestling of the ages shakes the hills of Tennessee,
With all their echoing mounts a-throb with war's wild minstrelsy;
A galaxy of stars new-born round the shield of Mars,
And set against the Stars and Stripes the flashing Stars and Bars.

'Twas Albert Sidney Johnston led the columns of the Gray,
Like Hector on the plains of Troy his presence fired the fray;
And dashing horse and gleaming sword spake out his royal will
As on the slopes of Shiloh field the blasts of war blew shrill.

"Down with the base invaders," the Gray shout forth the cry,
"Death to presumptuous rebels," the Blue ring out reply;
All day the conflict rages and yet again all day,
Though Grant is on the Union side he cannot stem nor stay.

They are a royal race of men, these brothers face to face,
Their fury speaking through their guns, their frenzy in their pace;
The sweeping onset of the Gray bears down the sturdy Blue,
Though Sherman and his legions are heroes through and through.

Though Prentiss and his gallant men are forcing scaur and crag,
They fall like sheaves before the scythes of Hardee and of Bragg;
Ah, who shall tell the victor's tale when all the strife is past,
When, man and man, in one great mould the men who strive are
    cast.

As when the Trojan hero came from that fair city's gates,
With tossing mane and flaming crest to scorn the scowling fates,
His legions gather round him and madly charge and cheer,
And fill the besieging armies with wild disheveled fear;

Then bares his breast unto the dart the daring spearsman sends,
And dying hears his cheering foes, the wailing of his friends,
So Albert Sidney Johnston, the chief of belt and scar,
Lay down to die at Shiloh and turned the scales of war.

Now five and twenty years are gone, and lo, to-day they come,
The Blue and Gray in proud array with throbbing fife and drum;
But not as rivals, not as foes, as brothers reconciled,
To twine love's fragrant roses where the thorns of hate grew wild.

They tell the hero of three wars, the lion-hearted man,
Who wore his valor like a star—uncrowned American;
Above his heart serene and still the folded Stars and Bars,
Above his head, like mother-wings, the sheltering Stripes and Stars.

Aye, five and twenty years, and lo, the manhood of the South
Has held its valor stanch and strong as at the cannon's mouth,
With patient heart and silent tongue has kept its true parole,
And in the conquests born of peace has crowned its battle roll.

But ever while we sing of war, of courage tried and true,
Of heroes wed to gallant deeds, or be it Gray or Blue,
Then Albert Sidney Johnston's name shall flash before our sight
Like some resplendent meteor across the sombre night.

America, thy sons are knit with sinews wrought of steel,
They will not bend, they will not break, beneath the tyrant's heel;
But in the white-hot flame of love, to silken cobwebs spun,
They whirl the engines of the world, all keeping time as one.

To-day they stand abreast and strong, who stood as foes of yore,
The world leaps up to bless their feet, heaven scatters blessings o'er;
Their robes are wrought of gleaming gold, their wings are
    freedom's own,
The trampling of their conquering hosts shakes pinnacle and throne.

Oh, veterans of the Blue and Gray, who fought on Shiloh field,
The purposes of God are true. His judgment stands revealed;
The pangs of war have rent the veil, and lo, His high decree:
One heart, one hope, one destiny, one flag from sea to sea.

THOMAS AT CHICKAMAUGA

Kate Brownlee Sherwood

★ ★ ★ ★ ★ ★

It was that fierce contested field when Chickamauga lay
Beneath the wild tornado that swept her pride away;
Her dimpling dales and circling hills dyed crimson with the flood
That had its sources in the springs that throb with human blood.

"Go say to General Hooker to reinforce his right!"
Said Thomas to his aide-de-camp, when wildly went the fight;
In front the battle thundered, it roared both right and left,
But like a rock "Pap" Thomas stood upon the crested cleft.

"Where will I find you, General, when I return?" The aide
Leaned on his bridle-rein to wait the answer Thomas made;
The old chief like a lion turned, his pale lips set and sere,
And shook his mane, and stamped his foot, and fiercely answered,
  "Here!"

The floodtide of fraternal strife rolled upward to his feet,
And like the breakers on the shore the thunderous clamors beat;
The sad earth rocked and reeled with woe, the woodland shrieked
    in pain,
And hill and vale were groaning with the burden of the slain.

Who does not mind that sturdy form, that steady heart and hand,
That calm repose and gallant mien, that courage high and grand?—
O God, who givest nations men to meet their lofty needs,
Vouchsafe another Thomas when our country prostrate bleeds!

They fought with all the fortitude of earnest men and true—
The men who wore the rebel gray, the men who wore the blue;
And those, they fought most valiantly for petty state and clan,
And these, for truer Union and the brotherhood of man.

They come, those hurling legions, with banners crimson-splashed,
Against our stubborn columns their rushing ranks are dashed,
Till 'neath the blistering iron hail the shy and frightened deer
Go scurrying from their forest haunts to plunge in wilder fear.

Beyond, our lines are broken; and now in frenzied rout
The flower of the Cumberland has swiftly faced about;
And horse and foot and color-guard are reeling, rear and van,
And in the awful panic man forgets that he is man.

Now Bragg, with pride exultant above our broken wings,
The might of all his army against "Pap" Thomas brings;
They're massing to the right of him, they're massing to the left,
Ah, God be with our hero, who holds the crested cleft!

Blow, blow, ye echoing bugles! give answer, screaming shell!
Go, belch your murderous fury, ye batteries of hell!
Ring out, O impious musket! spin on, O shattering shot,—
Our smoke-encircled hero, he hears but heeds ye not!

Now steady, men! now steady! make one more valiant stand,
For gallant Steedman's coming, his forces well in hand!
Close up your shattered columns, take steady aim and true,
The chief who loves you as his life will live or die with you!

By solid columns, on they come; by columns they are hurled,
As down the eddying rapids the storm-swept booms are whirled;
And when the ammunition fails—O moment drear and dread—
The heroes load their blackened guns from rounds of soldiers dead.

God never set His signet on the hearts of braver men,
Or fixed the goal of victory on higher heights than then;
With bayonets and muskets clubbed, they close the rush and roar;
Their stepping-stones to glory are their comrades gone before.

O vanished majesty of days not all forgotten yet,
We consecrate unto thy praise one hour of deep regret;
One hour to them whose days were years of glory that shall flood
The Nation's sombre night of tears, of carnage, and of blood!

O vanished majesty of days, when men were gauged by worth,
Set crowned and dowered in the way to judge the sons of earth;
When all the little great fell down before the great unknown,
And priest put off the hampering gown and coward donned his
      own!

O vanished majesty of days that saw the sun shine on
The deeds that wake sublimer praise than Ghent or Marathon;
When patriots in homespun rose—where one was called for, ten—
And heroes sprang full-armored from the humblest walks of men!

O vanished majesty of days! Rise, type and mould to-day,
And teach our sons to follow on where duty leads the way;
That whatsoever trial comes, defying doubt and fear,
They in the thickest fight shall stand and proudly answer, *"Here!"*

FARRAGUT

William Tuckey Meredith (dates unknown)

★ ★ ★ ★ ★ ★

Farragut, Farragut,
  Old Heart of Oak,
Daring Dave Farragut,
  Thunderbolt stroke,
Watches the hoary mist
  Lift from the bay,
Till his flag, glory-kissed,
  Greets the young day.

Far, by gray Morgan's walls,
  Looms the black fleet.
Hark, deck to rampart calls
  With the drums' beat!
Buoy your chains overboard,
  While the steam hums;
Men! to the battlement,
  Farragut comes.

See, as the hurricane
  Hurtles in wrath
Squadrons of clouds amain
  Back from its path!
Back to the parapet,
  To the guns' lips,
Thunderbolt Farragut
  Hurls the black ships.

Now through the battle's roar
   Clear the boy sings,
"By the mark fathoms four,"
   While his lead swings.
Steady the wheelmen five
   "Nor' by East keep her."
"Steady," but two alive:
   How the shells sweep her!

Lashed to the mast that sways
   Over red decks,
Over the flame that plays
   Round the torn wrecks,
Over the dying lips
   Framed for a cheer,
Farragut leads his ships,
   Guides the line clear.

On by heights cannon-browed,
   While the spars quiver;
Onward still flames the cloud
   Where the hulks shiver.
See, yon fort's star is set,
   Storm and fire past.
Cheer him, lads—Farragut,
   Lashed to the mast!

Oh! while Atlantic's breast
   Bears a white sail,
While the Gulf's towering crest
   Tops a green vale,
Men thy bold deeds shall tell,
   Old Heart of Oak,
Daring Dave Farragut,
   Thunderbolt stroke!

SHERMAN
Richard Watson Gilder (1844–1909)

★ ★ ★ ★ ★ ★

Glory and honor and fame and everlasting laudation
For our captains who loved not war, but fought for the life of the
nation;
Who knew that, in all the land, one slave meant strife, not peace;
Who fought for freedom, not glory; made war that war might
cease.

Glory and honor and fame; the beating of muffled drums;
The wailing funeral dirge, as the flag-wrapped coffin comes;
Fame and honor and glory; and joy for a noble soul,
For a full and splendid life, and laurelled rest at the goal.

Glory and honor and fame; the pomp that a soldier prizes;
The league-long waving line as the marching falls and rises;
Rumbling of caissons and guns; the clatter of horses' feet,
And a million awe-struck faces far down the waiting street.

But better than martial woe, and the pageant of civic sorrow;
Better than praise of to-day, or the statue we build to-morrow;
Better than honor and glory, and history's iron pen,
Was the thought of duty done and the love of his fellow-men.

ON A GREAT WARRIOR
Henry Abbey (1842–1911)

When all the sky was wild and dark,
  When every heart was wrung with fear,
He rose serene, and took his place,
  The great occasion's mighty peer.
He smote armed opposition down,
  He bade the storm and darkness cease,
And o'er the long-distracted land
  Shone out the smiling sun of peace.

The famous captains of the past
  March in review before the mind;
Some fought for glory, some for gold,
  But most to yoke and rule mankind.
Not so the captain, great of soul,
  At peace within his granite grave;
He fought to keep the Union whole,
  And break the shackles of the slave.

A silent man, in friendship true,
  He made point-blank his certain aim,
And, born a stranger to defeat,
  To steadfast purpose linked his name.
He followed duty with the mien
  Of but a soldier in the ranks,
This God-sent man that saved the State,
  And conquered its victorious thanks.

How well he wore white honor's flower,
    The gratitude and praise of men,
As General, as President,
    And then as simple citizen!
He was a hero to the end!
    The dark rebellion raised by death
Against the powers of life and light,
    He battled hard, with failing breath.

O hero of Fort Donelson,
    And wooded Shiloh's frightful strife!
Sleep on! for honor loves the tomb
    More than the garish ways of life.
Sleep on! sleep on! Thy wondrous days
    Fill freedom's most illustrious page.
Long-mem'ried Fame shall sound thy praise
    In every clime, in every age.

ROBERT E. LEE
Julia Ward Howe (1819–1910)

A gallant foeman in the fight,
    A brother when the fight was o'er,
The hand that led the host with might
    The blessed torch of learning bore.

No shriek of shells nor roll of drums,
    No challenge fierce, resounding far,
When reconciling Wisdom comes
    To heal the cruel wounds of war.

Thought may the minds of men divide,
    Love makes the heart of nations one,
And so, thy soldier grave beside,
    We honor thee, Virginia's son.

AN ODE IN TIME OF HESITATION

William Vaughn Moody (1869–1910)

★ ★ ★ ★ ★ ★ ★

I

Before the solemn bronze Saint Gaudens made
To thrill the heedless passer's heart with awe,
And set here in the city's talk and trade
To the good memory of Robert Shaw,
This bright March morn I stand,
And hear the distant spring come up the land;
Knowing that what I hear is not unheard
Of this boy soldier and his negro band,
For all their gaze is fixed so stern ahead,
For all the fatal rhythm of their tread.
The land they died to save from death and shame
Trembles and waits, hearing the spring's great name,
And by her pangs these resolute ghosts are stirred.

II

Through street and mall the tides of people go
Heedless; the trees upon the Common show
No hint of green; but to my listening heart
The still earth doth impart
Assurance of her jubilant emprise,
And it is clear to my long-searching eyes
That love at last has might upon the skies.
The ice is runneled on the little pond;
A telltale patter drips from off the trees;

99

The air is touched with southland spiceries,
As if but yesterday it tossed the frond
Of pendent mosses where the live-oaks grow
Beyond Virginia and the Carolines,
Or had its will among the fruits and vines
Of aromatic isles asleep beyond
Florida and the Gulf of Mexico.

III

Soon shall the Cape Ann children shout in glee,
Spying the arbutus, spring's dear recluse;
Hill lads at dawn shall hearken the wild goose
Go honking northward over Tennessee;
West from Oswego to Sault Sainte-Marie,
And on to where the Pictured Rocks are hung,
And yonder where, gigantic, willful, young,
Chicago sitteth at the northwest gates,
With restless violent hands and casual tongue
Moulding her mighty fates,
The Lakes shall robe them in ethereal sheen;
And like a larger sea, the vital green
Of springing wheat shall vastly be outflung
Over Dakota and the prairie states.
By desert people immemorial
On Arizona mesas shall be done
Dim rites unto the thunder and the sun;
Nor shall the primal gods lack sacrifice
More splendid, when the white Sierras call
Unto the Rockies straightway to arise
And dance before the unveiled ark of the year,
Sounding their windy cedars as for shawms,
Unrolling rivers clear
For flutter of broad phylacteries;

While Shasta signals to Alaskan seas
That watch old sluggish glaciers downward creep
To fling their icebergs thundering from the steep,
And Mariposa through the purple calms
Gazes at far Hawaii crowned with palms
Where East and West are met,—
A rich seal on the ocean's bosom set
To say that East and West are twain,
With different loss and gain:
The Lord hath sundered them; let them be sundered yet.

IV

Alas! what sounds are these that come
Sullenly over the Pacific seas,—
Sounds of ignoble battle, striking dumb
The season's half-awakened ecstasies?
Must I be humble, then,

Great wine of battle wrath by God's ring-finger stirred
Then upward, where the shadowy bastion loomed
Huge on the mountain in the wet sea light,
Whence now, and now, infernal flowerage bloomed,
Bloomed, burst, and scattered down its deadly seed,—
They swept, and died like freemen on the height,
Like freemen, and like men of noble breed;
And when the battle fell away at night
By hasty and contemptuous hands were thrust
Obscurely in a common grave with him
The fair-haired keeper of their love and trust.
Now limb doth mingle with dissolvèd limb
In nature's busy old democracy
To flush the mountain laurel when she blows
Sweet by the southern sea,

And heart with crumbled heart climbs in the rose:—
The untaught hearts with the high heart that knew
This mountain fortress for no earthly hold
Of temporal quarrel, but the bastion old
Of spiritual wrong,
Built by an unjust nation sheer and strong,
Expugnable but by a nation's rue
And bowing down before that equal shrine
By all men held divine,
Whereof his band and he were the most holy sign.

V

Lies! lies! It cannot be! The wars we wage
Are noble, and our battles still are won
By justice for us, ere we lift the gage.
We have not sold our loftiest heritage.
The proud republic hath not stooped to cheat
And scramble in the market-place of war;
Her forehead weareth yet its solemn star.
Here is her witness: this, her perfect son,
This delicate and proud New England soul
Who leads despised men, with just-unshackled feet,
Up the large ways where death and glory meet,
To show all peoples that our shame is done,
That once more we are clean and spirit-whole.

VI

Crouched in the sea fog on the moaning sand
All night he lay, speaking some simple word
From hour to hour to the slow minds that heard,
Holding each poor life gently in his hand
And breathing on the base rejected clay
Till each dark face shone mystical and grand
Against the breaking day;

And lo, the shard the potter cast away
Was grown a fiery chalice, crystal-fine,
Fulfilled of the divine
Great wine of battle wrath by God's ring-finger stirred.
Then upward, where the shadowy bastion loomed
Huge on the mountain in the wet sea light,
Whence now, and now, infernal flowerage bloomed,
Bloomed, burst, and scattered down its deadly seed,—
They swept, and died like freemen on the height,
Like freemen, and like men of noble breed;
And when the battle fell away at night
By hasty and contemptuous hands were thrust
Obscurely in a common grave with him
The fair-haired keeper of their love and trust.
Now limb doth mingle with dissolvèd limb
In nature's busy old democracy
To flush the mountain laurel when she blows
Sweet by the southern sea,
And heart with crumbled heart climbs in the rose:—
The untaught hearts with the high heart that knew
This mountain fortress for no earthly hold
Of temporal quarrel, but the bastion old
Of spiritual wrong,
Built by an unjust nation sheer and strong,
Expugnable but by a nation's rue
And bowing down before that equal shrine
By all men held divine,
Whereof his band and he were the most holy sign.

VII

O bitter, bitter shade!
Wilt thou not put the scorn
And instant tragic question from thine eyes?
Do thy dark brows yet crave

That swift and angry stave—
Unmeet for this desirous morn—
That I have striven, striven to evade?
Gazing on him, must I not deem they err
Whose careless lips in street and shop aver
As common tidings, deeds to make his cheek
Flush from the bronze, and his dead throat to speak?
Surely some elder singer would arise,
Whose harp hath leave to threaten and to mourn
Above this people when they go astray.
Is Whitman, the strong spirit, overworn?
Has Whittier put his yearning wrath away?
I will not and I dare not yet believe!
Though furtively the sunlight seems to grieve,
And the spring-laden breeze
Out of the gladdening west is sinister
With sounds of nameless battle overseas;
Though when we turn and question in suspense
If these things be indeed after these ways,
And what things are to follow after these,
Our fluent men of place and consequence
Fumble and fill their mouths with hollow phrase,
Or for the end-all of deep arguments
Intone their dull commercial liturgies—
I dare not yet believe! My ears are shut!
I will not hear the thin satiric praise
And muffled laughter of our enemies,
Bidding us never sheathe our valiant sword
Till we have changed our birthright for a gourd
Of wild pulse stolen from a barbarian's hut;
Showing how wise it is to cast away
The symbols of our spiritual sway,
That so our hands with better ease
May wield the driver's whip and grasp the jailer's keys.

VIII

Was it for this our fathers kept the law?
This crown shall crown their struggle and their ruth?
Are we the eagle nation Milton saw
Mewing its mighty youth,
Soon to possess the mountain winds of truth,
And be a swift familiar of the sun
Where aye before God's face his trumpets run?
Or have we but the talons and the maw,
And for the abject likeness of our heart
Shall some less lordly bird be set apart?—
Some gross-billed wader where the swamps are fat?
Some gorger in the sun? Some prowler with the bat?

IX

Ah no!
We have not fallen so.
We are our fathers' sons: let those who lead us know!
'T was only yesterday sick Cuba's cry

Came up the tropic wind, "Now help us, for we die!"
Then Alabama heard,
And rising, pale, to Maine and Idaho
Shouted a burning word.
Proud state with proud impassioned state conferred,
And at the lifting of a hand sprang forth,
East, west, and south, and north,
Beautiful armies. Oh, by the sweet blood and young
Shed on the awful hill slope at San Juan,
By the unforgotten names of eager boys
Who might have tasted girls' love and been stung
With the old mystic joys
And starry griefs, now the spring nights come on,

But that the heart of youth is generous,—
We charge you, ye who lead us,
Breathe on their chivalry no hint of stain!
Turn not their new-world victories to gain!
One least leaf plucked for chaffer from the bays
Of their dear praise,
One jot of their pure conquest put to hire,
The implacable republic will require;
With clamor, in the glare and gaze of noon,
Or subtly, coming as a thief at night,
But surely, very surely, slow or soon
That insult deep we deeply will requite.
Tempt not our weakness, our cupidity!
For save we let the island men go free,
Those baffled and dislaureled ghosts
Will curse us from the lamentable coasts
Where walk the frustrate dead.
The cup of trembling shall be drainèd quite,
Eaten the sour bread of astonishment,
With ashes of the hearth shall be made white
Our hair, and wailing shall be in the tent;
Then on your guiltier head
Shall our intolerable self-disdain
Wreak suddenly its anger and its pain;
For manifest in that disastrous light
We shall discern the right
And do it, tardily.—O ye who lead,
Take heed!
Blindness we may forgive, but baseness we will smite.

GETTYSBURG

Vicksburg capitulated on the 4th, compelled by the presence of absolute famine. This blow was harder on our citizens, even, than the reported repulse of Lee [*at Gettysburg*].
—*Southern Illustrated News,* July 1863

The Union victory at Gettysburg, together with the fall of Vicksburg, was a critical turning point in the war. Although almost two more years of fighting would pass before the bitter end, Lee had been prevented from penetrating too deeply into northern territory. The opportunity for swift Confederate success—and British diplomatic recognition of the Confederacy as a nation, which might well have changed the entire composition of the war—passed into history. The price was high for all concerned: 23,000 Union casualties and 28,000 Confederate men dead or out of action.[3]

"Gettysburg" by James Jeffrey Roche was composed for the dedication of the High Water Mark Monument on July 2, 1892, in commemoration of the dead at Gettysburg. Francis Bret Harte's "John Burns of Gettysburg" is a narrative celebration of one of the living legends of the war. According to a common saying, farmer John Burns was seventy years old on July 1, 1863, when he first borrowed a rifle and asked to be given a place in the battle of Gettysburg at the point of heaviest fighting in the line. The battle won, John Burns "Shouldered his rifle, unbent his brows, and then went back to his bees and cows."

Will Henry Thompson, author of "The High Tide at Gettysburg," was a Confederate soldier in the Fourth Georgia. His dramatic poem recalls the bold and ultimately disastrous charge made by George Pickett's Virginia division on the third day of the battle on July 3, 1863.

[3]McPherson, *Battle Cry of Freedom,* 664.

George Parsons Lathrop composed "Gettysburg: A Battle Ode" for the Society of the Army of the Potomac. It was read at the reunion of Confederate survivors on July 3, 1888, the twenty-fifth anniversary of Gettysburg.

GETTYSBURG

James Jeffrey Roche (1847–1908)

* * * * * *

There was no union in the land,
   Though wise men labored long
With links of clay and ropes of sand
   To bind the right and wrong.

There was no temper in the blade
   That once could cleave a chain;
Its edge was dull with touch of trade
   And clogged with rust of gain.

The sand and clay must shrink away
   Before the lava tide:
By blows and blood and fire assay
   The metal must be tried.

Here sledge and anvil met, and when
   The furnace fiercest roared,
God's undiscerning workingmen
   Reforged His people's sword.

Enough for them to ask and know
   The moment's duty clear—
The bayonets flashed it there below,
   The guns proclaimed it here:

To do and dare, and die at need,
　　But while life lasts, to fight—
For right or wrong a simple creed,
　　But simplest for the right.

They faltered not who stood that day
　　And held this post of dread;
Nor cowards they who wore the gray
　　Until the gray was red.

For every wreath the victor wears
　　The vanquished half may claim;
Every monument declares
　　A common pride and fame.

We raise no altar stones to Hate,
　　Who never bowed to Fear:
No province crouches at our gate,
　　To shame our triumph here.

Here standing by a dead wrong's grave
　　The blindest now may see,
The blow that liberates the slave
　　But sets the master free!

When ills beset the nation's life
　　Too dangerous to bear,
The sword must be the surgeon's knife,
　　Too merciful to spare.

O Soldier of our common land,
　　'Tis thine to bear that blade
Loose in the sheath, or firm in hand,
　　But ever unafraid.

When foreign foes assail our right,
One nation trusts to thee—
To wield it well in worthy fight—
The sword of Meade and Lee!

JOHN BURNS OF GETTYSBURG

Francis Bret Harte

Have you heard the story that gossips tell
Of Burns of Gettysburg? No? Ah, well:
Brief is the glory that hero earns,
Briefer the story of poor John Burns:
He was the fellow who won renown,—
The only man who didn't back down
When the rebels rode through his native town;
But held his own in the fight next day,
When all his townsfolk ran away.
That was in July, sixty-three,—
The very day that General Lee,
Flower of Southern chivalry,
Baffled and beaten, backward reeled
From a stubborn Meade and a barren field.

I might tell how, but the day before,
John Burns stood at his cottage-door,
Looking down the village street,
Where, in the shade of his peaceful vine,
He heard the low of his gathered kine,
And felt their breath with incense sweet;
Or I might say, when the sunset burned
The old farm gable, he thought it turned
The milk that fell like a babbling flood
Into the milk-pail, red as blood!
Or how he fancied the hum of bees

Were bullets buzzing among the trees.
But all such fanciful thoughts as these
Were strange to a practical man like Burns,
Who minded only his own concerns,
Troubled no more by fancies fine
Than one of his calm-eyed, long-tailed kine,
Quite old-fashioned and matter-of-fact,
Slow to argue, but quick to act.
That was the reason, as some folks say,
He fought so well on that terrible day.

And it was terrible. On the right
Raged for hours the heady fight,
Thundered the battery's double bass,—
Difficult music for men to face;
While on the left—where now the graves
Undulate like the living waves
That all the day unceasing swept
Up to the pits the rebels kept—
Round-shot ploughed the upland glades,
Sown with bullets, reaped with blades;
Shattered fences here and there,
Tossed their splinters in the air;
The very trees were stripped and bare;
The barns that once held yellow grain
Were heaped with harvests of the slain;
The cattle bellowed on the plain,
The turkeys screamed with might and main,
And the brooding barn-fowl left their rest
With strange shells bursting in each nest.

Just where the tide of battle turns,
Erect and lonely, stood old John Burns.
How do you think the man was dressed?
He wore an ancient, long buff vest,

Yellow as saffron,—but his best;
And, buttoned over his manly breast,
Was a bright blue coat with a rolling collar,
And large gilt buttons,—size of a dollar,—
With tails that the country-folk called "swaller."
He wore a broad-brimmed, bell-crowned hat,
White as the locks on which it sat.
Never had such a sight been seen
For forty years on the village green,
Since old John Burns was a country beau,
And went to the "quiltings" long ago.

Close at his elbows all that day
Veterans of the Peninsula,
Sunburnt and bearded, charged away;
And striplings, downy of lip and chin,—
Clerks that the Home-Guard mustered in,—
Glanced, as they passed, at the hat he wore,
Then at the rifle his right hand bore;
And hailed him, from out their youthful lore,
With scraps of a slangy repertoire:
"How are you, White Hat?" "Put her through!"
"Your head's level!" and "Bully for you!"
Called him "Daddy,"—begged he'd disclose
The name of the tailor who made his clothes,
And what was the value he set on those;
While Burns, unmindful of jeer and scoff,
Stood there picking the rebels off,—
With his long brown rifle, and bell-crowned hat,
And the swallow-tails they were laughing at.

'Twas but a moment, for that respect
Which clothes all courage their voices checked;
And something the wildest could understand
Spake in the old man's strong right hand,

And his corded throat, and the lurking frown
Of his eyebrows under his old bell-crown;
Until, as they gazed, there crept an awe
Through the ranks in whispers, and some men saw,
In the antique vestments and long white hair,
The Past of the Nation in battle there;
And some of the soldiers since declare
That the gleam of his old white hat afar,
Like the crested plume of the brave Navarre,
That day was their oriflamme of war.

So raged the battle. You know the rest:
How the rebels, beaten and backward pressed,
Broke at the final charge and ran.
At which John Burns—a practical man—
Shouldered his rifle, unbent his brows,
And then went back to his bees and cows.

That is the story of old John Burns;
This is the moral the reader learns:
In fighting the battle, the question's whether
You'll show a hat that's white or a feather.

THE HIGH TIDE
AT GETTYSBURG

Will Henry Thompson (dates unknown)

★　★　★　★　★　★

A cloud possessed the hollow field,
The gathering battle's smoky shield:
   Athwart the gloom the lightning flashed,
   And through the cloud some horsemen dashed,
And from the heights the thunder pealed.

Then, at the brief command of Lee,
Moved out that matchless infantry,
   With Pickett leading grandly down,
   To rush against the roaring crown
Of those dread heights of destiny.

Far heard above the angry guns
A cry across the tumult runs,—
   The voice that rang through Shiloh's woods
   And Chickamauga's solitudes,
The fierce South cheering on her sons!

Ah, how the withering tempest blew
Against the front of Pettigrew!
   A Khamsin wind that scorched and singed
   Like that infernal flame that fringed
The British squares at Waterloo!

A thousand fell where Kemper led;
A thousand died where Garnett bled:
   In blinding flame and strangling smoke
   The remnant through the batteries broke
And crossed the works with Armistead.

"Once more in Glory's van with me!"
Virginia cried to Tennessee;
   "We two together, come what may,
   Shall stand upon these works to-day!"
(The reddest day in history.)

Brave Tennessee! In reckless way
Virginia heard her comrade say:
   "Close round this rent and riddled rag!"
   What time she set her battle-flag
Amid the guns of Doubleday.

But who shall break the guards that wait
Before the awful face of Fate?
   The tattered standards of the South
   Were shrivelled at the cannon's mouth,
And all her hopes were desolate.

In vain the Tennesseean set
His breast against the bayonet;
   In vain Virginia charged and raged,
   A tigress in her wrath uncaged,
Till all the hill was red and wet!

Above the bayonets, mixed and crossed,
Men saw a gray, gigantic ghost
   Receding through the battle-cloud,
   And heard across the tempest loud
The death-cry of a nation lost!

The brave went down! Without disgrace
They leaped to Ruin's red embrace;
   They only heard Fame's thunders wake,
   And saw the dazzling sun-burst break
In smiles on Glory's bloody face!

They fell, who lifted up a hand
And bade the sun in heaven to stand;
   They smote and fell, who set the bars
   Against the progress of the stars,
And stayed the march of Motherland!

They stood, who saw the future come
On through the fight's delirium;
   They smote and stood, who held the hope
   Of nations on that slippery slope
Amid the cheers of Christendom.

God lives! He forged the iron will
That clutched and held that trembling hill!
   God lives and reigns! He built and lent
   The heights for freedom's battlement
Where floats her flag in triumph still!

Fold up the banners! Smelt the guns!
Love rules. Her gentler purpose runs.
   A mighty mother turns in tears
   The pages of her battle years,
Lamenting all her fallen sons!

GETTYSBURG: A BATTLE ODE

George Parsons Lathrop

★ ★ ★ ★ ★ ★ ★

Victors, living, with laureled brow,
  And you that sleep beneath the sward!
Your song was poured from cannon throats:
It rang in deep-tongued bugle-notes:
Your triumph came; you won your crown,
The grandeur of a word's renown.
      But, in our later days,
      Full freighted with your praise,
Fair memory harbors those whose lives, laid down
  In gallant faith and generous heat,
    Gained only sharp defeat.
All are at peace, who once so fiercely warred:
Brother and brother, now, we chant a common chord.

      For, if we say God wills,
      Shall we then idly deny Him
      Care of each host in the fight?
      His thunder was here in the hills
      When the guns were loud in July;
      And the flash of the musketry's light
      Was sped by a ray from God's eye.
      In its good and its evil the scheme
      Was framed with omnipotent hand,
      Though the battle of men was a dream
      That they could but half understand.

Can the purpose of God pass by him?
   Nay; it was sure, and was wrought
Under inscrutable powers:
   Bravely the two armies fought
And left the land, that was greater than they,
   Still theirs and ours!

Lucid, pure, and calm and blameless
   Dawned on Gettysburg the day
That should make the spot, once fameless,
   Known to nations far away.
Birds were caroling, and farmers
   Gladdened o'er their garnered hay,
When the clank of gathering armors
   Broke the morning's peaceful sway;
And the living lines of foemen
   Drawn o'er pasture, brook, and hill,
Formed in figures weird of omen
   That should work with mystic will
Measures of a direful magic—
   Shattering, maiming—and should fill
Glades and gorges with a tragic
   Madness of desire to kill.
Skirmishers flung lightly forward
   Moved like scythemen skilled to sweep
Westward o'er the field and nor'ward,
   Death's first harvest there to reap.
You would say the soft, white smoke-puffs
   Were but languid clouds asleep,
Here on meadows, there on oak-bluffs,
   Fallen foam of Heaven's blue deep.
Yet that blossom-white outbreaking
   Smoke wove soon a martyr's shroud.
Reynolds fell, with soul unquaking,
   Ardent-eyed and open-browed:

Noble men in humbler raiment
　　Fell where shot their graves had plowed,
Dying not for paltry payment:
　　Proud of home, of honor proud.

. . . .

　　　　Dear are the dead we weep for;
　　　　Dear are the strong hearts broken!
　　　　Proudly their memory we keep for
　　　　Our help and hope; a token
　　　　Of sacred thought too deep for
　　　　Words that leave it unspoken.
　　　　All that we know of fairest,
　　　　All that we have of meetest,
　　　　Here we lay down for the rarest
　　　　Doers whose souls rose fleetest
　　　　And in their homes of air rest,
　　　　Ranked with the truest and sweetest.

Days, with fiery-hearted, bold advances;
　　Nights in dim and shadowy, swift retreat;
Rains that rush with bright, embattled lances;
　　Thunder, booming round your stirless feet;—
Winds that set the orchard with sweet fancies
　　All abloom, or ripple the ripening wheat;
Moonlight, starlight, on your mute graves falling;
　　Dew, distilled as tears unbidden flow;—
Dust of drought in drifts and layers crawling;
　　Lulling dreams of softly whispering snow:
Happy birds, from leafy coverts calling;—
　　These go on, yet none of these you know:
　　　　Hearing not our human voices
　　　　Speaking to you all in vain,
　　　　Nor the psalm of a land that rejoices,

Ringing from churches and cities and foundries
    a mighty refrain!
But we, and the sun and the birds, and the breezes
    that blow
When tempests are striving and lightnings of heaven
    are spent,
With one consent make unto them who died for us
    eternal requiem.

Lovely to look on, O South,
No longer stately-scornful
    But beautiful still in pride,
Our hearts go out to you as toward a bride!
    Garmented soft in white,
Haughty, and yet how love-imbuing and tender!
You stand before us with your gently mournful
Memory-haunted eyes and flower-like mouth
Where clinging thoughts—as bees a-cluster
Murmur through the leafy gloom,
    Musical in monotone—
Whisper sadly.
Yet a luster as of glowing gold-gray light
    Shines upon the orient bloom,
    Sweet with orange-blossoms, thrown
Round the jasmine-starred, deep night
Crowning with dark hair your brow.
Ruthless, once, we came to slay,
    And you met us then with hate.
Rough was the wooing of war: we won you,
    Won you at last, though late!
Dear South, to-day,
As our country's altar made us
    One forever, so we vow
Unto yours our love to render:
Strength with strength we here endow,

And we make your honor ours.
Happiness and hope shall sun you:
All the wiles that half betrayed us
Vanish from us like spent showers.

Two hostile bullets in mid-air
Together shocked,
And swift were locked
Forever in a firm embrace.
Then let us men have so much grace
To take the bullet's place,
And learn that we are held
By laws that weld
Our hearts together!
As once we battled hand to hand,
So hand in hand to-day we stand,
Sworn to each other,
Brother and brother,
In storm and mist, or calm, translucent weather:
And Gettysburg's guns, with their death-giving roar,
Echoed from ocean to ocean, shall pour
Quickening life to the nation's core;
Filling our minds again
With the spirit of those who wrought in the
Field of the Flower of Men!

THE END
OF THE
STRUGGLE

When Lee surrendered to Grant at Appomattox on April 9, 1865, he put an end to the bloodiest war in American history. Politically, economically, and personally, peace came as a relief to both sides. The period of recovery and Reconstruction found some regional spirit still firmly intact even in a shattered land; the North and the South set about rebuilding the nation and these poems reveal the mixed feelings of that time.

"Acceptation" by Margaret Junkin Preston expresses the necessity of meeting the present conditions head on—in the context of the memories of a glorious past. Preston's close association with both Stonewall Jackson and Robert E. Lee gave her the courage and voice to speak for the South as a whole.

In a departure from the usual humorous vein, Francis Bret Harte's "A Second Review of the Grand Army" is trenchant and grieving. Harte's response to The Grand Review is a ghostly parade of martyred heroes and nameless dead—a direct strike against the famous celebration of May 23–24, 1865, in which the 200,000 men of The Army of the Potomac and Sherman's Army of Georgia marched down Pennsylvania Avenue before demobilization. Kate Putnam Osgood's "Driving Home the Cows" voices the anxiety of both Northerners and Southerners as they waited for news of family and friends at the end of the war. The high mortality rate in Southern prisons only contributed further to the distress of those awaiting the release of a prisoner of war.

In "After All," William Winter mourns the losses of the cruel war. Abram Joseph Ryan, author of "The Conquered Banner," was a Confederate chaplain. Ryan wrote this popular poem that laments the weary subjugation of the South to the Union while the news of Lee's surrender was still fresh in his heart.

ACCEPTATION

Margaret Junkin Preston

★ ★ ★ ★ ★ ★ ★

We do accept thee, heavenly Peace!
  Albeit thou comest in a guise
  Unlooked for—undesired, our eyes
Welcome through tears the sweet release
From war, and woe, and want,—surcease,
For which we bless thee, blessèd Peace!

We lift our foreheads from the dust;
  And as we meet thy brow's clear calm,
  There falls a freshening sense of balm
Upon our spirits. Fear—distrust—
The hopeless present on us thrust—
We'll meet them as we can, and *must*.

War has not wholly wrecked us: still
  Strong hands, brave hearts, high souls are ours—
  Proud consciousness of quenchless powers—
A Past whose memory makes us thrill—
Futures uncharactered, to fill
With heroisms—if we will.

Then courage, brothers!—Though each breast
  Feel oft the rankling thorn, despair,
  That failure plants so sharply there—
No pain, no pang shall be confest:
We'll work and watch the brightening west,
And leave to God and Heaven the rest.

127

A SECOND REVIEW OF THE GRAND ARMY

Francis Bret Harte

I read last night of the Grand Review
   In Washington's chiefest avenue,—
Two hundred thousand men in blue,
   I think they said was the number,—
Till I seemed to hear their trampling feet,
The bugle blast and the drum's quick beat,
The clatter of hoofs in the stony street,
The cheers of the people who came to greet,
And the thousand details that to repeat
   Would only my verse encumber,—
Till I fell in a revery, sad and sweet,
   And then to a fitful slumber.

When, lo! in a vision I seemed to stand
In the lonely Capitol. On each hand
Far stretched the portico, dim and grand
Its columns ranged, like a martial band
Of sheeted spectres whom some command
   Had called to a last reviewing.
And the streets of the city were white and bare;
No footfall echoed across the square;
But out of the misty midnight air
I heard in the distance a trumpet blare,
And the wandering night-winds seemed to bear
   The sound of a far tattooing.

Then I held my breath with fear and dread;
For into the square, with a brazen tread,
There rode a figure whose stately head
    O'erlooked the review that morning,
That never bowed from its firm-set seat
When the living column passed its feet,
Yet now rode steadily up the street
    To the phantom bugle's warning:

Till it reached the Capitol square, and wheeled,
And there in the moonlight stood revealed
A well known form that in State and field
    Had led our patriot sires:
Whose face was turned to the sleeping camp,
Afar through the river's fog and damp,
That showed no flicker, nor waning lamp,
    Nor wasted bivouac fires.

And I saw a phantom army come,
With never a sound of fife or drum,
But keeping time to a throbbing hum
    Of wailing and lamentation:
The martyred heroes of Malvern Hill,
Of Gettysburg and Chancellorsville,
The men whose wasted figures fill
    The patriot graves of the nation.

And there came the nameless dead,—the men
Who perished in fever-swamp and fen,
The slowly-starved of the prison-pen;
    And marching beside the others,
Came the dusky martyrs of Pillow's fight,
With limbs enfranchised and bearing bright:
I thought—perhaps 'twas the pale moonlight—
    They looked as white as their brothers!

And so all night marched the Nation's dead,
With never a banner above them spread,
Nor a badge, nor a motto brandishèd;
No mark—save the bare uncovered head
  Of the silent bronze Reviewer;
With never an arch save the vaulted sky;
With never a flower save those that lie
On the distant graves—for love could buy
  No gift that was purer or truer.

So all night long swept the strange array;
So all night long, till the morning gray,
I watch'd for one who had passed away,
  With a reverent awe and wonder,—
Till a blue cap waved in the lengthening line,
And I knew that one who was kin of mine
Had come; and I spake—and lo! that sign
  Awakened me from my slumber.

DRIVING HOME THE COWS
Kate Putnam Osgood (1841–?)

Out of the clover and blue-eyed grass
   He turned them into the river-lane;
One after another he let them pass,
   Then fastened the meadow-bars again.

Under the willows, and over the hill,
   He patiently followed their sober pace;
The merry whistle for once was still,
   And something shadowed the sunny face.

Only a boy! and his father had said
   He never could let his youngest go:
Two already were lying dead
   Under the feet of the trampling foe.

But after the evening work was done,
   And the frogs were loud in the meadow-swamp,
Over his shoulder he slung his gun,
   And stealthily followed the foot-path damp,

Across the clover, and through the wheat,
   With resolute heart and purpose grim,
Though cold was the dew on his hurrying feet,
   And the blind bat's flitting startled him.

Thrice since then had the lanes been white,
   And the orchards sweet with apple-bloom;
And now, when the cows came back at night,
   The feeble father drove them home.

For news had come to the lonely farm
   That three were lying where two had lain;
And the old man's tremulous, palsied arm
   Could never lean on a son's again.

The summer day grew cool and late.
   He went for the cows when the work was done;
But down the lane, as he opened the gate,
   He saw them coming one by one,—

Brindle, Ebony, Speckle, and Bess,
   Shaking their horns in the evening wind;
Cropping the buttercups out of the grass,—
   But who was it following close behind?

Loosely swung in the idle air
   The empty sleeve of army blue;
And worn and pale, from the crisping hair,
   Looked out a face that the father knew.

For Southern prisons will sometimes yawn,
   And yield their dead unto life again;
And the day that comes with a cloudy dawn
   In golden glory at last may wane.

The great tears sprang to their meeting eyes;
   For the heart must speak when the lips are dumb:
And under the silent evening skies
   Together they followed the cattle home.

AFTER ALL
William Winter (1836–1917)

★ ★ ★ ★ ★ ★

The apples are ripe in the orchard,
  The work of the reaper is done,
And the golden woodlands redden
  In the blood of the dying sun.

At the cottage-door the grandsire
  Sits pale in his easy-chair,
While the gentle wind of twilight
  Plays with his silver hair.

A woman is kneeling beside him;
  A fair young head is pressed,
In the first wild passion of sorrow,
  Against his aged breast.

And far from over the distance
  The faltering echoes come
Of the flying blast of trumpet
  And the rattling roll of drum.

And the grandsire speaks in a whisper:
  "The end no man can see;
But we give him to his country,
  And we give our prayers to Thee."

The violets star the meadows,
   The rose-buds fringe the door,
And over the grassy orchard
   The pink-white blossoms pour.

But the grandsire's chair is empty,
   The cottage is dark and still;
There's a nameless grave in the battle-field,
   And a new one under the hill.

And a pallid, tearless woman
   By the cold hearth sits alone;
And the old clock in the corner
   Ticks on with a steady drone.

THE CONQUERED BANNER
Abram Joseph Ryan (1838–1886)

Furl that Banner, for 'tis weary;
Round its staff 'tis drooping dreary;
   Furl it, fold it—it is best;
For there's not a man to wave it,
And there's not a sword to save it,
And there's not one left to lave it
In the blood which heroes gave it;
And its foes now scorn and brave it;
   Furl it, hide it—let it rest!

Take that Banner down! 'tis tattered;
Broken is its staff and shattered;
And the valiant hosts are scattered,
   Over whom it floated high.
Oh, 'tis hard for us to fold it,
Hard to think there's none to hold it,
Hard that those who once unrolled it
   Now must furl it with a sigh!

Furl that Banner—furl it sadly;
Once ten thousands hailed it gladly,
And ten thousands wildly, madly,
   Swore it should forever wave—
Swore that foeman's sword should never
Hearts like theirs entwined dissever,
Till that flag should float forever
   O'er their freedom or their grave!

135

Furl it! for the hands that grasped it,
And the hearts that fondly clasped it,
　　Cold and dead are lying low;
And that Banner—it is trailing,
While around it sounds the wailing
　　Of its people in their woe.

For, though conquered, they adore it—
Love the cold, dead hands that bore it!
Weep for those who fell before it!
Pardon those who trailed and tore it!
But, oh, wildly they deplore it,
　　Now who furl and fold it so!

Furl that Banner! True, 'tis gory,
Yet 'tis wreathed around with glory,
And 'twill live in song and story
　　Though its folds are in the dust!
For its fame on brightest pages,
Penned by poets and by sages,
Shall go sounding down the ages—
　　Furl its folds though now we must.

Furl that Banner, softly, slowly;
Treat it gently—it is holy,
　　For it droops above the dead;
Touch it not—unfold it never;
Let it droop there, furled forever,—
　　For its people's hopes are fled.

LINCOLN

On April 14, 1865, President Abraham Lincoln was assassinated by John Wilkes Booth. Tragedy had struck a nation barely reunited; even while Confederate troops were still surrendering, Grant wept over Lincoln's body as he lay in state.

Walt Whitman's "O Captain! My Captain!" is the best of the Lincoln eulogies—much anthologized, and occasionally taken outside of historical context, this famous poem merits a close historical and literary reading.

Richard Watson Gilder's "On the Life-Mask of Abraham Lincoln" was directly inspired by a facsimile of Lincoln's life-mask that Gilder kept in his editorial offices at the *Century Magazine*. Another type of "statue" poem, where the soul of the man is drawn from the statue by the poet, is Edmund Clarence Stedman's "The Hand of Lincoln."

Richard Henry Stoddard's "Abraham Lincoln" laments the remarkable man who undertook to lead a divided nation. His weighty poem measures the stages of national grief—astonishment at the loss, plunge into deep mourning, recognition of the extraordinary period when the rebellious South had finally been subdued, a grim funeral procession, and the quiet, honored grave. At the time he wrote this poem, Stoddard had already made his reputation as a literary reviewer for *The New York World*.

On July 21, 1865, Harvard College held commemorative services for students and graduates killed in the war. James Russell Lowell, Smith Professor of Modern Languages at Harvard, was selected to compose the official poem, the "Ode Recited at the Harvard Commemoration." Although his ode was not particularly well received on that occasion, Lowell later became firmly established as the preeminent poet of American patriotism.

O CAPTAIN! MY CAPTAIN!

Walt Whitman

★ ★ ★ ★ ★ ★ ★

O Captain! my Captain! our fearful trip is done,
The ship has weathered every rack, the prize we sought is won,
The port is near, the bells I hear, the people all exulting,
While follow eyes the steady keel, the vessel grim and daring;
  But O heart! heart! heart!
    O the bleeding drops of red,
      Where on the deck my Captain lies,
        Fallen cold and dead.

O Captain! my Captain! rise up and hear the bells;
Rise up—for you the flag is flung—for you the bugle trills,
For you bouquets and ribboned wreaths—for you the shores
    a-crowding
For you they call, the swaying mass, their eager faces turning;
  Here Captain! dear father!
    This arm beneath your head!
      It is some dream that on the deck
        You've fallen cold and dead.

My Captain does not answer, his lips are pale and still,
My father does not feel my arm, he has no pulse nor will,
The ship is anchored safe and sound, its voyage closed and done,
From fearful trip the victor ship comes in with object won;
  Exult O shores, and ring O bells!
    But I, with mournful tread,
      Walk the deck my Captain lies,
        Fallen cold and dead.

ON THE LIFE-MASK
OF ABRAHAM LINCOLN

Richard Watson Gilder

★ ★ ★ ★ ★ ★

This bronze doth keep the very form and mould
Of our great martyr's face. Yes, this is he:
That brow all wisdom, all benignity;
That human, humorous mouth; those cheeks that hold
Like some harsh landscape all the summer's gold;
That spirit fit for sorrow, as the sea
For storms to beat on; the lone agony
Those silent, patient lips too well foretold.
Yes, this is he who ruled a world of men
As might some prophet of the elder day—
Brooding above the tempest and the fray
With deep-eyed thought and more than mortal ken,
A power was his beyond the touch of art
Or armèd strength—his pure and mighty heart.

THE HAND OF LINCOLN
Edmund Clarence Stedman

★ ★ ★ ★ ★ ★ ★

Look on this cast, and know the hand
   That bore a nation in its hold:
From this mute witness understand
   What Lincoln was,—how large of mould.

The man who sped the woodsman's team,
   And deepest sunk the ploughman's share,
And pushed the laden raft astream,
   Of fate before him unaware.

This was the hand that knew to swing
   The axe—since thus would Freedom train
Her son—and made the forest ring,
   And drove the wedge, and toiled amain.

Firm hand, that loftier office took,
   A conscious leader's will obeyed,
And, when men sought his word and look,
   With steadfast might the gathering swayed.

No courtier's, toying with a sword,
   Nor minstrel's, laid across a lute;
A chief's uplifted to the Lord
   When all the kings of earth were mute!

The hand of Anak, sinewed strong,
　　The fingers that on greatness clutch;
Yet, lo! the marks their lines along
　　Of one who strove and suffered much.

For here in knotted cord and vein
　　I trace the varying chart of years;
I know the troubled heart, the strain,
　　The weights of Atlas—and the tears.

Again I see the patient brow
　　That palm erewhile was wont to press;
And now 't is furrowed deep, and now
　　Made smooth with hope and tenderness.

For something of a formless grace
　　This moulded outline plays about;
A pitying flame, beyond our trace,
　　Breathes like a spirit, in and out,—

The love that cast an aureole
　　Round one who, longer to endure,
Called mirth to ease his ceaseless dole,
　　Yet kept his nobler purpose sure.

Lo, as I gaze, the statured man,
　　Built up from yon large hand, appears:
A type that Nature wills to plan
　　But once in all a people's years.

What better than this voiceless cast
　　To tell of such a one as he,
Since through its living semblance passed
　　The thought that bade a race be free!

ABRAHAM LINCOLN
Richard Henry Stoddard (1825–1903)

★ ★ ★ ★ ★ ★

Not as when some great Captain falls
In battle, where his Country calls,
   Beyond the struggling lines
   That push his dread designs

To doom, by some stray ball struck dead:
Or, in the last charge, at the head
   Of his determined men,
   Who *must* be victors then.

Nor as when sink the civic great,
The safer pillars of the State,
   Whose calm, mature, wise words
   Suppress the need of swords.

With no such tears as e'er were shed
Above the noblest of our dead
   Do we to-day deplore
   The Man that is no more.

Our sorrow hath a wider scope,
Too strange for fear, too vast for hope,
   A wonder, blind and dumb,
   That waits—what is to come!

Not more astounded had we been
If Madness, that dark night, unseen,
   Had in our chambers crept,
   And murdered while we slept!

We woke to find a mourning earth,
Our Lares shivered on the hearth,
   The roof-tree fallen, all
   That could affright, appall!

Such thunderbolts, in other lands,
Have smitten the rod from royal hands,
   But spared, with us, till now,
   Each laureled Cæsar's brow.

No Cæsar he whom we lament,
A Man without a precedent,
   Sent, it would seem, to do
   His work, and perish, too.

Not by the weary cares of State,
The endless tasks, which will not wait,
   Which, often done in vain,
   Must yet be done again:

Not in the dark, wild tide of war,
Which rose so high, and rolled so far,
   Sweeping from sea to sea
   In awful anarchy:

Four fateful years of mortal strife,
Which slowly drained the nation's life,
   (Yet for each drop that ran
   There sprang an armèd man!)

Not then; but when, by measures meet,
By victory, and by defeat,
   By courage, patience, skill,
   The people's fixed *"We will!"*

Had pierced, had crushed Rebellion dead,
Without a hand, without a head,
   At last, when all was well,
   He fell, O how he fell!

The time, the place, the stealing shape,
The coward shot, the swift escape,
   The wife—the widow's scream,—
   It is a hideous Dream!

A dream? What means this pageant, then?
These multitudes of solemn men,
   Who speak not when they meet,
   But throng the silent street?

The flags half-mast that late so high
Flaunted at each new victory?
   (The stars no brightness shed,
   But bloody looks the red!)

The black festoons that stretch for miles,
And turn the streets to funeral aisles?
   (No house too poor to show
   The nation's badge of woe.)

The cannon's sudden, sullen boom,
The bells that toll of death and doom,
   The rolling of the drums,
   The dreadful car that comes?

Cursed be the hand that fired the shot,
The frenzied brain that hatched the plot,
  Thy country's Father slain
  By thee, thou worse than Cain!

Tyrants have fallen by such as thou,
And good hath followed—may it now!
  (God lets bad instruments
  Produce the best events.)

But he, the man we mourn to-day,
No tyrant was: so mild a sway
  In one such weight who bore
  Was never known before.

Cool should he be, of balanced powers,
The ruler of a race like ours,
  Impatient, headstrong, wild,
  The Man to guide the Child.

And this *he* was, who most unfit
(So hard the sense of God to hit),
  Did seem to fill his place;
  With such a homely face,

Such rustic manners, speech uncouth,
(That somehow blundered out the truth),
  Untried, untrained to bear
  The more than kingly care.

Ah! And his genius put to scorn
The proudest in the purple born,
  Whose wisdom never grew
  To what, untaught, he knew,

The People, of whom he was one:
No gentleman, like Washington,
   (Whose bones, methinks, make room,
   To have him in their tomb!)

A laboring man, with horny hands,
Who swung the ax, who tilled his lands,
   Who shrank from nothing new,
   But did as poor men do.

One of the People! Born to be
Their curious epitome;
   To share yet rise above
   Their shifting hate and love.

O honest face, which all men knew!
O tender heart, but known to few!
   O wonder of the age,
   Cut off by tragic rage!

Peace! Let the long procession come,
For hark, the mournful, muffled drum,
   The trumpet's wail afar,
   And see, the awful car!

Peace! Let the sad procession go,
While cannon boom and bells toll slow.
   And go, thou sacred car,
   Bearing our woe afar!

Go, darkly borne, from State to State,
Whose loyal, sorrowing cities wait
   To honor all they can
   The dust of that good man.

Go, grandly borne, with such a train
As greatest kings might die to gain.
   The just, the wise, the brave,
   Attend thee to the grave.

And you, the soldiers of our wars,
Bronzed veterans, grim with noble scars,
   Salute him once again,
   Your late commander—slain!

So sweetly, sadly, sternly goes
The Fallen to his last repose.
   Beneath no mighty dome,
   But in his modest home;

The churchyard where his children rest,
The quiet spot that suits him best,
   There shall his grave be made,
   And there his bones be laid.

And there his countrymen shall come,
With memory proud, with pity dumb,
   And strangers far and near,
   For many and many a year.

For many a year and many an age,
While History on her ample page
   The virtues shall enroll
   Of that Paternal Soul.

ODE RECITED AT THE HARVARD COMMEMORATION

James Russell Lowell (1819–1891)

★ ★ ★ ★ ★ ★ ★

Such was he, our Martyr-Chief,
 Whom late the Nation he had led,
 With ashes on her head,
Wept with the passion of an angry grief:
Forgive me, if from present things I turn
To speak what in my heart will beat and burn,
And hang my wreath on his world-honored urn.
 Nature, they say, doth dote,
 And cannot make a man
 Save on some worn-out plan,
 Repeating us by rote:
For him her Old-World moulds aside she threw,
 And, choosing sweet clay from the breast
 Of the unexhausted West,
With stuff untainted shaped a hero new,
Wise, steadfast in the strength of God, and true.
 How beautiful to see
Once more a shepherd of mankind indeed,
Who loved his charge, but never loved to lead;
One whose meek flock the people joyed to be,
 Not lured by any cheat of birth,
 But by his clear-grained human worth,
And brave old wisdom of sincerity!
 They knew that outward grace is dust;

They could not choose but trust
In that sure-footed mind's unfaltering skill,
   And supple-tempered will
That bent like perfect steel to spring again and thrust.
   His was no lonely mountain-peak of mind,
   Thrusting to thin air o'er our cloudy bars,
   A sea-mark now, now lost in vapors blind;
   Broad prairie rather, genial, level-lined,
   Fruitful and friendly for all human kind,
Yet also nigh to heaven and loved of loftiest stars.
   Nothing of Europe here,
Or, then, of Europe fronting mornward still,
   Ere any names of Serf and Peer
   Could Nature's equal scheme deface
   And thwart her genial will;
   Here was a type of the true elder race,
And one of Plutarch's men talked with us face to face.
   I praise him not; it were too late;
And some innative weakness there must be
In him who condescends to victory
Such as the Present gives, and cannot wait,
   Safe in himself as in a fate.
      So always firmly he:
      He knew to bide his time
      And can his fame abide,
Still patient in his simple faith sublime,
   Till the wise years decide.
Great captains, with their guns and drums,
   Disturb our judgment for the hour,
      But at last silence comes;
These are all gone, and standing like a tower,
Our children shall behold his fame,
   The kindly-earnest, brave, foreseeing man,
Sagacious, patient, dreading praise, not blame,
New birth of our new soil, the first American.

   .   .   .   .   .

  Not in anger, not in pride,
  Pure from passion's mixture rude
  Ever to base earth allied,
  But with far-heard gratitude,
  Still with heart and voice renewed,
To heroes living and dear martyrs dead,
The strain should close that consecrates our brave.
Lift the heart and lift the head!
  Lofty be its mood and grave,
  Not without a martial ring,
  Not without a prouder tread
  And a peal of exultation:
  Little right has he to sing
  Through whose heart in such an hour
  Beats no march of conscious power,
  Sweeps no tumult of elation!
  'Tis no Man we celebrate,
  By his country's victories great,
  A hero half, and half the whim of Fate,
  But the pith and marrow of a Nation
  Drawing force from all her men,
  Highest, humblest, weakest, all,
  For her time of need, and then
  Pulsing it again through them,
Till the basest can no longer cower,
Feeling his soul spring up divinely tall,
Touched but in passing by her mantle-hem.
Come back, then, noble pride, for 'tis her dower!
  How could poet ever tower,
  If his passions, hopes, and fears,
  If his triumphs and his tears,
  Kept not measure with his people?
Boom, cannon, boom to all the winds and waves!
Clash out, glad bells, from every rocking steeple!

Banners, advance with triumph, bend your staves!
    And from every mountain-peak
    Let beacon-fire to answering beacon speak,
    Katahdin tell Monadnock, Whiteface he,
And so leap on in light from sea to sea,
    Till the glad news be sent
    Across a kindling continent,
Making earth feel more firm and air breathe braver:
"Be proud! for she is saved, and all have helped to save her!
    She that lifts up the manhood of the poor,
    She of the open soul and open door,
    With room about her hearth for all mankind!
    The fire is dreadful in her eyes no more;
    From her bold front the helm she doth unbind,
    Sends all her handmaid armies back to spin,
    And bids her navies, that so lately hurled
    Their crashing battle, hold their thunders in,
    Swimming like birds of calm along the unharmful shore.
    No challenge sends she to the elder world,
    That looked askance and hated; a light scorn
    Plays o'er her mouth, as round her mighty knees
    She calls her children back, and waits the morn
Of nobler day, enthroned between her subject seas."

THE
HERITAGE

Death was the common heritage of the Civil War. The poems in this section commemorate the men killed on both sides and gradually draw closer to the renewed spirit of freedom and national unity that was Lincoln's enduring endeavor.

Francis Miles Finch's national classic "The Blue and the Gray" was inspired by the following item in the New York *Tribune* of 1867: "The women of Columbus, Mississippi, animated by nobler sentiments than many of their sisters, have shown themselves impartial in their offerings made to the memory of the dead. They strewed flowers alike on the graves of the Confederate and of the National soldiers."

Walt Whitman's "When Lilacs Last in the Dooryard Bloom'd" also provided the text for a popular song by the same name. This epic poem runs from the familiar lines so often sung: "When lilacs last in the dooryard bloom'd, and the great star early droop'd in the western sky in the night, I mourn'd, and yet shall mourn with ever-returning spring," to the shattering verse: "I saw battle-corpses, myriads of them, and the white skeletons of young men, I saw them, I saw the débris and débris of all the slain soldiers of the war. . . ." Finally, for his ending, Whitman returns to the quiet, healing images of nature: "There in the fragrant pines and the cedars dusk and dim."

John Albee's "A Soldier's Grave" is a reminder that each Memorial Day brings thoughts of the lives lost in the service of the nation. Henry Timrod's "Ode at Magnolia Cemetery" was sung on Memorial Day in 1867, on the occasion of decorating the graves of the Confederate dead at Magnolia Cemetery in Charleston, South Carolina. Timrod was a native of Charleston whose fiery martial lyrics had inspired thousands of men to fight for the Confederacy.

"Over Their Graves" by Henry Jerome Stockyard points out that even nature cannot unbury the dead; Mary Ashley Townsend's "A

Georgia Volunteer" memorializes the grave of the unknown Georgia volunteer. Henry Peterson's "Ode for Decoration Day" unites North and South by declaring that "in the realms of Sorrow all are friends." "The Tournament" by Sidney Lanier is a revision of Lanier's previous poem "The Psalm of the West"; this version is known as one of the earliest southern poems to express a true feeling of national unity.

THE BLUE AND THE GRAY
Francis Miles Finch (1827–1907)

★ ★ ★ ★ ★ ★ ★

By the flow of the inland river,
   Whence the fleets of iron have fled,
Where the blades of the grave-grass quiver,
   Asleep are the ranks of the dead:
      Under the sod and the dew,
         Waiting the judgment-day;
      Under the one, the Blue,
         Under the other, the Gray.

These in the robings of glory,
   Those in the gloom of defeat,
All with the battle-blood gory,
   In the dusk of eternity meet:
      Under the sod and the dew,
         Waiting the judgment-day;
      Under the laurel, the Blue,
         Under the willow, the Gray.

From the silence of sorrowful hours
   The desolate mourners go,
Lovingly laden with flowers
   Alike for the friend and the foe:
      Under the sod and the dew,
         Waiting the judgment-day;
      Under the roses, the Blue,
         Under the lilies, the Gray.

So with an equal splendor,
  The morning sun-rays fall,
With a touch impartially tender,
  On the blossoms blooming for all:
    Under the sod and the dew,
      Waiting the judgment-day;
    Broidered with gold, the Blue,
      Mellowed with gold, the Gray.

So, when the summer calleth,
  On forest and field of grain,
With an equal murmur falleth
  The cooling drip of the rain:
    Under the sod and the dew,
      Waiting the judgment-day;
    Wet with the rain, the Blue,
      Wet with the rain, the Gray.

Sadly, but not with upbraiding,
  The generous deed was done,
In the storm of the years that are fading
  No braver battle was won:
    Under the sod and the dew,
      Waiting the judgment-day;
    Under the blossoms, the Blue,
      Under the garlands, the Gray.

No more shall the war cry sever,
  Or the winding rivers be red;
They banish our anger forever
  When they laurel the graves of our dead!
    Under the sod and the dew,
      Waiting the judgment-day;
    Love and tears for the Blue,
      Tears and love for the Gray.

WHEN LILACS LAST
IN THE DOORYARD BLOOM'D

Walt Whitman

★ ★ ★ ★ ★ ★ ★

I

When lilacs last in the dooryard bloom'd,
And the great star early droop'd in the western sky in the night,
I mourn'd, and yet shall mourn with ever-returning spring.

Ever-returning spring, trinity sure to me you bring,
Lilac blooming perennial and drooping star in the west,
And thought of him I love.

II

O powerful western fallen star!
O shades of night—O moody, tearful night!
O great star disappear'd—O the black murk that hides the star!
O cruel hands that hold me powerless—O helpless soul of me!
O harsh surrounding cloud that will not free my soul.

III

In the dooryard fronting an old farm-house near the white-wash'd
    palings,
Stands the lilac-bush tall-growing with heart-shaped leaves of rich
    green,
With many a pointed blossom rising delicate, with the perfume
    strong I love,

With every leaf a miracle—and from this bush in the door-yard,
With delicate-colour'd blossoms and heart-shaped leaves of rich
     green,
A sprig with its flower I break.

IV

In the swamp in secluded recesses,
A shy and hidden bird is warbling a song.

Solitary the thrush,
The hermit withdrawn to himself, avoiding the settlements,
Sings by himself a song.
Song of the bleeding throat,
Death's outlet song of life (for well dear brother I know,
If thou wast not granted to sing thou would'st surely die).

V

Over the breast of the spring, the land, amid cities,
Amid lanes and through old woods, where lately the violets peep'd
     from the ground, spotting the gray débris,
Amid the grass in the fields each side of the lanes, passing the
     endless grass,
Passing the yellow-spear'd wheat, every grain from its shroud in
     the dark-brown fields uprisen,
Passing the apple-tree blows of white and pink in the orchards,
Carrying a corpse to where it shall rest in the grave,
Night and day journeys a coffin.

VI

Coffin that passes through lanes and streets,
Through day and night with the great cloud darkening the land,
With the pomp of the inloop'd flags with the cities draped in
     black,

With the show of the States themselves as of crape-veil'd women
    standing,
With processions long and winding and the flambeaus of the night,
With the countless torches lit, with the silent sea of faces and the
    unbared heads,
With the waiting depot, the arriving coffin, and the sombre faces,
With dirges through the night, with the thousand voices rising
    strong and solemn,
With all the mournful voices of the dirges pour'd around the
    coffin,
The dim-lit churches and the shuddering organs—where amid these
    you journey,
With the tolling tolling bells' perpetual clang,
Here, coffin that slowly passes,
I give you my sprig of lilac.

VII

(Nor for you, for one alone,
Blossoms and branches green to coffins all I bring,
For fresh as the morning, thus would I chant a song for you O
    sane and sacred death.
All over bouquets of roses,
O death, I cover you over with roses and early lilies,
But mostly and now the lilac that blooms the first,
Copious I break, I break the sprigs from the bushes,
With loaded arms I come, pouring for you,
For you and the coffins all of you O death.)

VIII

O western orb sailing the heaven,
Now I know what you must have meant as a month since I
    walk'd,
As I walk'd in silence the transparent shadowy night,

As I saw you had something to tell as you bent to me night after
    night,
As you dropp'd from the sky low down as if to my side (while
    the other stars all look'd on),
As we wander'd together the solemn night (for something I know
    not what kept me from sleep),
As the night advanced, and I saw on the rim of the west how full
    you were of woe,
As I stood on the rising ground in the breeze in the cool
    transparent night,
As I watch'd where you pass'd and was lost in the netherward
    black of the night,
As my soul in its trouble dissatisfied sank, as where you sad orb,
Concluded, dropt in the night, and was gone.

IX

Sing on there in the swamp,
O singer bashful and tender, I hear your notes, I hear your call,
I hear, I come presently, I understand you,
But a moment I linger, for the lustrous star has detain'd me,
The star my departing comrade holds and detains me.

X

O how shall I warble myself for the dead one there I loved?
And how shall I deck my song for the large sweet soul that has
    gone?
And what shall my perfume be for the grave of him I love?

Sea-winds blown from east and west,
Blown from the Eastern sea and blown from the Western sea, till
    there on the prairies meeting,
These and with these and the breath of my chant,
I'll perfume the grave of him I love.

XI

O what shall I hang on the chamber walls?
And what shall the pictures be that I hang on the walls,
To adorn the burial-house of him I love?

Pictures of growing spring and farms and homes,
With the Fourth-month eve at sundown, and the gray smoke lucid
    and bright,
With floods of the yellow gold of the gorgeous, indolent, sinking
    sun, burning, expanding the air,
With the fresh sweet herbage under foot, and the pale green leaves
    of the trees prolific,
In the distance the flowing glaze, the breast of the river, with a
    wind-dapple here and there,
With ranging hills on the banks, with many a line against the sky,
    and shadows,
And the city at hand with dwellings so dense, and stacks of
    chimneys,
And all the scenes of life and the workshops, and the workmen
    homeward returning.

XII

Lo, body and soul—this land,
My own Manhattan with spires, and the sparkling and hurrying
    tides, and the ships,
The varied and ample land, the South and the North in the light,
    Ohio's shores and flashing Missouri,
And ever the far-spreading prairies cover'd with grass and corn.

Lo, the most excellent sun so calm and haughty,
The violet and purple morn with just-felt breezes,
The gentle soft-born measureless light,
The miracle spreading bathing all, the fulfill'd noon,

The coming eve delicious, the welcome night and the stars,
Over my cities shining all, enveloping man and land.

XIII

Sing on, sing on you gray-brown bird,
Sing from the swamps, the recesses, pour your chant from the
    bushes,
Limitless out of the dusk, out of the cedars and pines.
Sing on dearest brother, warble your reedy song,
Loud human song, with voice of uttermost woe.

O liquid and free and tender!
O wild and loose to my soul—O wondrous singer!
You only I hear—yet the star holds me (but will soon depart),
Yet the lilac with mastering odour holds me.

XIV

Now while I sat in the day and look'd forth,
In the close of the day with its light and the fields of spring, and
    the farmers preparing their crops,
In the large unconscious scenery of my land with its lakes and
    forests,
In the heavenly aerial beauty (after the perturb'd winds and the
    storms),
Under the arching heavens of the afternoon swift passing, and the
    voices of children and women,
The many-moving sea-tides, and I saw the ships how they sail'd,
And the summer approaching with richness, and the fields all busy
    with labour,
And the infinite separate houses, how they all went on, each with
    its meals and minutia of daily usages,
And the streets how their throbbings throbb'd, and the cities
    pent—lo, then and there,

Falling upon them all and among them all, enveloping me with the
    rest,
Appear'd the cloud, appear'd the long black trail,
And I knew death, its thought, and the sacred knowledge of death.

Then with the knowledge of death as walking one side of me,
And the thought of death close-walking the other side of me,
And I in the middle as with companions, and as holding the hands
    of companions,
I fled forth to the hiding receiving night that talks not,
Down to the shores of the water, the path by the swamp in the
    dimness,
To the solemn shadowy cedars and ghostly pines so still.

And the singer so shy to the rest receiv'd me,
The gray-brown bird I know receiv'd us comrades three,
And he sang the carol of death, and a verse for him I love.

From deep secluded recesses,
From the fragrant cedars and the ghostly pines so still,
Came the carol of the bird.

And the charm of the carol rapt me,
As I held as if by their hands my comrades in the night,
And the voice of my spirit tallied the song of the bird.

Come lovely and soothing death,
Undulate round the world, serenely arriving, arriving,
In the day, in the night, to all, to each,
Sooner or later delicate death.

Prais'd be the fathomless universe,
For life and joy, and for objects and knowledge curious,
And for love, sweet love—but praise! praise! praise!
For the sure-enwinding arms of cool-enfolding death.

Dark mother always gliding near with soft feet,
Have none chanted for thee a chant of fullest welcome?
Then I chant it for thee, I glorify thee above all,
I bring thee a song that when thou must indeed come, come
    unfalteringly.

Approach strong deliveress,
When it is so, when thou hast taken them I joyously sing the dead,
Lost in the loving floating ocean of thee,
Laved in the flood of thy bliss O death.

From me to thee glad serenades,
Dances for thee I propose saluting thee, adornments and feastings for
    thee,
And the sights of the open landscape and the high-spread sky are fitting,
And life and the fields, and the huge and thoughtful night.

The night in silence under many a star,
The ocean shore and the husky whispering wave whose voice I know,
And the soul turning to thee O vast and well-veil'd death,
And the body gratefully nestling close to thee.

Over the tree-tops I float thee a song,
Over the rising and sinking waves, over the myriad fields and the
    prairies wide,
Over the dense-pack'd cities all and the teeming wharves and ways,
I float this carol with joy, with joy to thee O death.

    XV

To the tally of my soul,
Loud and strong kept up the gray-brown bird,
With pure deliberate notes spreading filling the night.
Loud in the pines and cedars dim,

Clear in the freshness moist and the swamp-perfume,
And I with my comrades there in the night.

While my sight that was bound in my eyes unclosed,
As to long panoramas of visions.

And I saw askant the armies,
I saw as in noiseless dreams hundreds of battle-flags,
Borne through the smoke of the battles and pierc'd with missiles I
        saw them,
And carried hither and yon through the smoke, and torn and
        bloody,
And at last but a few shreds left on the staffs (and all in silence),
And the staffs all splinter'd and broken.

I saw battle-corpses, myriads of them,
And the white skeletons of young men, I saw them,
I saw the débris and débris of all the slain soldiers of the war,
But I saw they were not as was thought,
They themselves were fully at rest, they suffer'd not,
The living remain'd and suffer'd, the mother suffer'd,
And the wife and the child and the musing comrade suffer'd,
And the armies that remain'd suffer'd.

XVI

Passing the visions, passing the night,
Passing, unloosing the hold of my comrades' hands,
Passing the song of the hermit bird and the tallying song of my
        soul,
Victorious song, death's outlet song, yet varying ever-altering song,
As low and wailing, yet clear the notes, rising and falling, flooding
        the night,
Sadly sinking and fainting, as warning and warning, and yet again
        bursting with joy,

Covering the earth and filling the spread of the heaven,
As that powerful psalm in the night I heard from recesses,
Passing, I leave thee lilac with heart-shaped leaves,
I leave thee there in the dooryard, blooming, returning with
      spring.

I cease from my song for thee,
From my gaze on thee in the west, fronting the west, communing
      with thee,
O comrade lustrous with silver face in the night.

Yet each to keep and all, retrievements out of the night,
The song, the wondrous chant of the gray-brown bird,
And the tallying chant, the echo arous'd in my soul,
With the lustrous and drooping star with the countenance full of
      woe,
With the holders holding my hand nearing the call of the bird,
Comrades mine and I in the midst, and their menory ever to keep,
      for the dead I loved so well,
For the sweetest, wisest soul of all my days and lands—and this for
      his dear sake,
Lilac and star and bird twined with the chant of my soul,
There in the fragrant pines and the cedars dusk and dim.

A SOLDIER'S GRAVE

John Albee (1833–1911)

Break not his sweet repose—
Thou whom chance brings to this sequestered ground,
The sacred yard his ashes close,
But go thy way in silence; here no sound
Is ever heard but from the murmuring pines,
   Answering the sea's near murmur;
   Nor ever here comes rumor
Of anxious world or war's foregathering signs.
   The bleaching flag, the faded wreath,
   Mark the dead soldier's dust beneath,
   And show the death he chose;
Forgotten save by her who weeps alone,
And wrote his fameless name on this low stone:
   Break not his sweet repose.

ODE AT MAGNOLIA CEMETERY

Henry Timrod

Sleep sweetly in your humble graves,
　　Sleep, martyrs of a fallen cause;
Though yet no marble column craves
　　The pilgrim here to pause.

In seeds of laurel in the earth
　　The blossom of your fame is blown,
And somewhere, waiting for its birth,
　　The shaft is in the stone!

Meanwhile, behalf the tardy years
　　Which keep in trust your storied tombs,
Behold! your sisters bring their tears,
　　And these memorial blooms.

Small tributes! but your shades will smile
　　More proudly on these wreaths to-day,
Than when some cannon-moulded pile
　　Shall overlook this bay.

Stoop, angels, hither from the skies!
　　There is no holier spot of ground
Than where defeated valor lies,
　　By mourning beauty crowned.

OVER THEIR GRAVES

Henry Jerome Stockyard (dates unknown)

★ ★ ★ ★ ★ ★ ★

Over their graves rang once the bugle's call,
The searching shrapnel and the crashing ball;
   The shriek, the shock of battle, and the neigh
   Of horse; the cries of anguish and dismay;
And the loud cannon's thunders that appall.

Now through the years the brown pine-needles fall,
The vines run riot by the old stone wall,
   By hedge, by meadow streamlet, far away,
     Over their graves.

We love our dead where'er so held in thrall.
Than they no Greek more bravely died, nor Gaul—
   A love that's deathless!—but they look to-day
   With no reproaches on us when we say,
"Come, let us grasp your hands, we're brothers all,
     Over their graves!"

A GEORGIA VOLUNTEER

Mary Ashley Townsend (1832–1901)

Far up the lonely mountain-side
  My wandering footsteps led;
The moss lay thick beneath my feet,
  The pine sighed overhead.
The trace of a dismantled fort
  Lay in the forest nave,
And in the shadow near my path
  I saw a soldier's grave.

The bramble wrestled with the weed
  Upon the lowly mound;—
The simple head-board, rudely writ,
  Had rotted to the ground;
I raised it with a reverent hand,
  From dust its words to clear,
But time had blotted all but these—
  "A Georgia Volunteer!"

I saw the toad and scaly snake
  From tangled covert start,
And hide themselves among the weeds
  Above the dead man's heart;
But undisturbed, in sleep profound,
  Unheeding, there he lay;
His coffin but the mountain soil,
  His shroud Confederate gray.

I heard the Shenandoah roll
    Along the vale below,
I saw the Alleghanies rise
    Towards the realms of snow.
The "Valley Campaign" rose to mind—
    Its leader's name—and then
I knew the sleeper had been one
    Of Stonewall Jackson's men.

Yet whence he came, what lip shall say—
    Whose tongue will ever tell
What desolated hearths and hearts
    Have been because he fell?
What sad-eyed maiden braids her hair,
    Her hair which he held dear?
One lock of which perchance lies with
    The Georgia Volunteer!

What mother, with long watching eyes,
    And white lips cold and dumb,
Waits with appalling patience for
    Her darling boy to come?
Her boy! whose mountain grave swells up
    But one of many a scar,
Cut on the face of our fair land,
    By gory-handed war.

What fights he fought, what wounds he wore,
    Are all unknown to fame;
Remember, on his lonely grave
    There is not e'en a name!
That he fought well and bravely too,
    And held his country dear,
We know, else he had never been
    A Georgia Volunteer.

He sleeps—what need to question now
    If he were wrong or right?
He knows, ere this, whose cause was just
    In God the Father's sight.
He wields no warlike weapons now,
    Returns no foeman's thrust—
Who but a coward would revile
    An honest soldier's dust?

Roll, Shenandoah, proudly roll,
    Adown thy rocky glen,
Above thee lies the grave of one
    Of Stonewall Jackson's men.
Beneath the cedar and the pine,
    In solitude austere,
Unknown, unnamed, forgotten, lies
    A Georgia Volunteer.

ODE FOR DECORATION DAY
Henry Peterson (1818–1891)

★ ★ ★ ★ ★ ★

O gallant brothers of the generous South,
   Foes for a day and brothers for all time!
I charge you by the memories of our youth,
   By Yorktown's field and Montezuma's clime,
   Hold our dead sacred—let them quietly rest
In your unnumbered vales, where God thought best.
Your vines and flowers learned long since to forgive,
And o'er their graves a broidered mantle weave:
Be you as kind as they are, and the word
Shall reach the Northland with each summer bird,
And thoughts as sweet as summer shall awake
Responsive to your kindness, and shall make
Our peace the peace of brothers once again,
And banish utterly the days of pain.

And ye, O Northmen! be ye not outdone
   In generous thought and deed.
We all do need forgiveness, every one;
   And they that give shall find it in their need.
Spare of your flowers to deck the stranger's grave,
   Who died for a lost cause:—
A soul more daring, resolute, and brave,
   Ne'er won a world's applause.
A brave man's hatred pauses at the tomb.
For him some Southern home was robed in gloom,
Some wife or mother looked with longing eyes

Through the sad days and nights with tears and sighs,
Hope slowly hardening into gaunt Despair.
Then let your foeman's grave remembrance share:
Pity a higher charm to Valor lends,
And in the realms of Sorrow all are friends.

THE TOURNAMENT
Sidney Lanier

★ ★ ★ ★ ★ ★ ★

Lists all white and blue in the skies;
   And the people hurried amain
To the Tournament under the ladies' eyes
   Where jousted Heart and Brain.

Blow, Herald, blow! There entered Heart,
   A youth in crimson and gold.
Blow, Herald, blow! Brain stood apart,
   Steel-armored, glittering cold.

Heart's palfrey caracoled gayly round,
   Heart tra-li-raed merrily;
But Brain sat still, with never a sound—
   Full cynical-calm was he.

Heart's helmet-crest bore favors three
   From his lady's white hand caught;
Brain's casque was bare as Fact—not he
   Or favor gave or sought.

Blow, Herald, blow! Heart shot a glance
   To catch his lady's eye;
But Brain looked straight a-front, his lance
   To aim more faithfully.

They charged, they struck; both fell, both bled;
  Brain rose again, ungloved;
Heart fainting smiled, and softly said,
  "My love to my Beloved!"

    Heart and brain! No more be twain;
    Throb and think, one flesh again!
    Lo! they weep, they turn, they run;
    Lo! they kiss: Love, thou art one!

BROTHERHOOD

The arduous period of Reconstruction began while the North and South paid homage to their dead. Those still living had to come to terms with the past in the ugly face of the present. Reunion was a reality. The poems of this period are no longer voices whispering in the aftermath of a bloody peace, but the clarion cry of one nation reunited.

Walt Whitman's "Over the Carnage Rose Prophetic a Voice" celebrates the common bond and brotherhood of the land in an emotional poem written rather earlier than its theme came to pass. John Jerome Rooney, author of "Joined the Blues," found his entertaining verse much appreciated by the real General "Joe" Wheeler in his poem, so much so that Rooney and Wheeler later became close friends.

A generation after the Civil War, the Spanish War of 1898 proved that some of the enmities of the 1860s had disappeared. Men who had once fought against each other now battled together for common principles of freedom; this is the subject of Wallace Rice's "Wheeler's Brigade at Santiago."

The inspiration for "Those Rebel Flags" by John Howard Hewitt was the agitation for captured Confederate battle flags held by the War Department in Washington to be returned to their respective states. A bill authorizing this action was passed unanimously on February 24, 1905.

Frank Lebby Stanton's "One Country" is a remarkable example of how far the North and South had progressed since the war days. Stanton, a native of South Carolina (the first state to secede from the Union), wrote this poem in 1898, advocating one country "Against the foes of liberty and God!"

OVER THE CARNAGE
ROSE PROPHETIC A VOICE
Walt Whitman

★ ★ ★ ★ ★ ★ ★

Over the carnage rose prophetic a voice,
Be not dishearten'd, affection shall solve the
    problems of freedom yet,
Those who love each other shall become invincible,
They shall yet make Columbia victorious.

Sons of the Mother of All, you shall yet be victorious,
You shall yet laugh to scorn the attacks of all
    the remainder of the earth.

No danger shall balk Columbia's lovers,
If need be a thousand shall sternly immolate
    themselves for one.

One from Massachusetts shall be a Missourian's comrade,
From Maine and from hot Carolina, and another
    an Oregonese, shall be friends triune,
More precious to each other than all the
    riches of the earth.

To Michigan, Florida perfumes shall tenderly come,
Not the perfumes of flowers, but sweeter, and
    wafted beyond death.

It shall be customary in the houses and
    streets to see manly affection,
The most dauntless and rude shall touch face
    to face lightly,
The dependence of Liberty shall be lovers,
The continuance of Equality shall be comrades.

These shall tie you and band you stronger
    than hoops of iron,
I, ecstatic, O partners! O lands! with the love
    of lovers tie you.

(Were you looking to be held together by lawyers?
Or by an agreement on a paper? or by arms?
Nay, nor the world, nor any living thing, will so cohere.)

JOINED THE BLUES

John Jerome Rooney (dates unknown)

* * * * * * *

Says Stonewall Jackson to "Little Phil": "Phil, have you heard the
    news?
Why, our 'Joe' Wheeler—'Fighting Joe'—has gone and joined the
    blues.

"Ay, no mistake—I saw him come—I heard the oath he took—
And you'll find it duly entered up in yon great Record Book.

"Yes, 'Phil,' it is a change since then (we give the Lord due
    thanks)
When 'Joe' came swooping like a hawk upon your Sherman's
    flanks!

"Why, 'Phil,' you knew the trick yourself—but 'Joe' had all the
    points—
And we've yet to hear his horses died of stiff or rusty joints!

"But what of that?—the deed I saw to-day in yonder town
Leads all we did and all 'Joe' did in troopings up and down;

"For, 'Phil,' that oath shall be the heal of many a bleeding wound,
And many a Southland song shall yet to that same oath be tuned!

"The oath 'Joe' swore has done the work of thrice a score of
    years—
Ay, more than oath—he swore away mistrust and hate and tears!"

"Yes, yes," says "Phil," "he was, indeed, a right good worthy foe,
And well he knew, in those fierce days, to give us blow for blow.

"When 'Joe' came round to pay a call—the commissaries said—
Full many a swearing, grumbling 'Yank' went supperless to bed:

"He seemed to have a pesky knack—so Sherman used to say—
Of calling, when he should by rights be ninety miles away!

"Come, Stonewall, put your hand in mine,—'Joe's sworn old
      Samuel's oath—
We're never North or South again—he kissed the Book for both!"

WHEELER'S BRIGADE AT SANTIAGO

Wallace Rice (1859–1939)

★　★　★　★　★　★　★

'Neath the lances of the tropic sun
　　The column is standing ready,
Awaiting the fateful command of one
　　　Whose word will ring out
　　　To an answering shout
　　To prove it alert and steady.
And a stirring chorus all of them sung
　　With singleness of endeavor,
Though some to "The Bonny Blue Flag" had swung
　　And some to "The Union For Ever."

The order came sharp through the desperate air
　　And the long ranks rose to follow,
Till their dancing banners shone more fair
　　　Than the brightest ray
　　　Of the Cuban day
　　On the hill and jungled hollow;
And to "Maryland" some in the days gone by
　　Had fought through the combat's rumble,
And some for "Freedom's Battle-Cry"
　　Had seen the broad earth crumble.

Full many a widow weeps in the night
　　Who had been a man's wife in the morning;
For the banners we loved we bore to the height

185

Where the enemy stood
As a hero should,
His valor his country adorning;
But drops of pride with your tears of grief,
Ye American women, mix ye!
For the North and South, with a Southern chief,
Kept time to the tune of "Dixie."

THOSE REBEL FLAGS

John Howard Jewett (1843–1925)

★ ★ ★ ★ ★ ★ ★

Shall we send back the Johnnies their bunting,
  In token, from Blue to the Gray,
That "Brothers-in-blood" and "Good Hunting"
  Shall be our new watchword to-day?
In olden times knights held it knightly
  To return to brave foemen the sword;
Will the Stars and the Stripes gleam less brightly
  If the old Rebel flags are restored?

Call it sentiment, call it misguided
  To fight to the death for "a rag";
Yet, trailed in the dust, derided,
  The true soldier still loves his flag!
Does love die, and must honor perish
  When colors and causes are lost?
Lives the soldier who ceases to cherish
  The blood-stains and valor they cost?

Our battle-fields, safe in the keeping
  Of Nature's kind, fostering care,
Are blooming,—our heroes are sleeping,—
  And peace broods perennial there.
All over our land rings the story
  Of loyalty, fervent and true;
"One flag," and that flag is "Old Glory,"
  Alike for the Gray and the Blue.

Why cling to those moth-eaten banners?
  What glory or honor to gain
While the nation is shouting hosannas,
  Uniting her sons to fight Spain?
Time is ripe, and the harvest worth reaping,
  Send the Johnnies their flags f.o.b.,
Address to the care and safe keeping
  Of that loyal "old Reb," Fitzhugh Lee!

Yes, send back the Johnnies their bunting,
  With greetings from Blue to the Gray;
We are "Brothers-in-blood," and "Good Hunting"
  Is America's watchword to-day.

ONE COUNTRY
Frank Lebby Stanton (1857–1927)

★ ★ ★ ★ ★ ★ ★

After all,
One country, brethren! We must rise or fall
With the Supreme Republic. We must be
The makers of her immortality,—
    Her freedom, fame,
    Her glory or her shame:
Liegemen to God and fathers of the free!

After all—
Hark! from the heights the clear, strong, clarion call
And the command imperious: "Stand forth,
Sons of the South and brothers of the North!
    Stand forth and be
    As one on soil and sea—
Your country's honor more than empire's worth!"

After all,
'Tis Freedom wears the loveliest coronal;
Her brow is to the morning; in the sod
She breathes the breath of patriots; every clod
    Answers her call
    And rises like a wall
Against the foes of liberty and God!

FAMOUS
LYRICS

O f all the poems and songs inspired by the Civil War, these famous lyrics have weathered time to become part of the most popular tradition.

In 1861, Julia Ward Howe was invited to a military review in the Virginia camps. Hearing her singing "John Brown's Body" on the way back, her pastor invited her to find better words for the melody. She wrote the "Battle-Hymn of the Republic" that evening. The sixth stanza of the song, although seldom quoted, is reproduced here. Howe's later life was devoted to the cause of women's suffrage.

James Ryder Randall held the Chair of English literature at Poydras College in Pointe Coupée, Louisiana, when he learned of Maryland's attack on the Sixth Massachusetts in Baltimore on April 19, 1861. That same night he wrote "My Maryland," which instantly became wildly popular throughout the South and was also liberally parodied in the North. First printed in the New Orleans *Delta* of April 26, 1861, "My Maryland" was immediately picked up by almost every southern journal. Randall wrote at that time, "There was borne to me, in my remote place of residence, evidence that I had made a great hit, and that, whatever might be the fate of the Confederacy, the song would survive it."

Sung to the tune of the popular song "Dixie," Albert Pike's version of "Dixie" enjoyed instant popularity throughout the South. (The Union version of "Dixie" may be found in the last chapter of this book.) In 1861, the first New Orleans performance of "Pocohantas" opened with a chorus singing "Dixie." Pike, a Boston-born lawyer, was the Confederate general who guaranteed the southern allegiance of the tribes in the Indian territory.

BATTLE-HYMN OF THE REPUBLIC

Julia Ward Howe

Mine eyes have seen the glory of the coming of the Lord:
He is trampling out the vintage where the grapes of wrath are
      stored;
He hath loosed the fateful lightning of his terrible swift sword:
    His truth is marching on.

I have seen Him in the watch-fires of a hundred circling camps;
They have builded Him an altar in the evening dews and damps;
I can read His righteous sentence by the dim and flaring lamps.
    His day is marching on.

I have read a fiery gospel, writ in burnished rows of steel:
"As ye deal with my contemners, so with you my grace shall deal;
Let the Hero, born of woman, crush the serpent with his heel,
    Since God is marching on."

He has sounded forth the trumpet that shall never call retreat;
He is sifting out the hearts of men before his judgment-seat:
Oh! be swift, my soul, to answer Him! be jubilant, my feet!
    Our God is marching on.

In the beauty of the lilies Christ was born across the sea,
With a glory in his bosom that transfigures you and me:
As He died to make men holy, let us die to make men free,
    While God is marching on.

He is coming like the glory of the morning on the wave,
He is wisdom to the mighty, he is honor to the brave,
So the world shall be his footstool, and the soul of wrong his
slave,
Our God is marching on!

MY MARYLAND

James Ryder Randall

★ ★ ★ ★ ★ ★

The despot's heel is on thy shore,
     Maryland!
His torch is at thy temple door,
     Maryland!
Avenge the patriotic gore
That flecked the streets of Baltimore,
And be the battle-queen of yore,
     Maryland, my Maryland!

Hark to an exiled son's appeal,
     Maryland!
My Mother State, to thee I kneel,
     Maryland!
For life and death, for woe and weal,
Thy peerless chivalry reveal,
And gird thy beauteous limbs with steel,
     Maryland, my Maryland!

Thou wilt not cower in the dust,
     Maryland!
Thy beaming sword shall never rust,
     Maryland!
Remember Carroll's sacred trust,
Remember Howard's warlike thrust,
And all thy slumberers with the just,
     Maryland, my Maryland!

Come! 'tis the red dawn of the day,
        Maryland!
Come with thy panoplied array,
        Maryland!
With Ringgold's spirit for the fray,
With Watson's blood at Monterey,
With fearless Lowe and dashing May,
        Maryland, my Maryland!

Come! for thy shield is bright and strong,
        Maryland!
Come! for thy dalliance does thee wrong,
        Maryland!
Come to thine own heroic throng,
Stalking with Liberty along,
And chant thy dauntless slogan-song,
        Maryland, my Maryland!

Dear Mother, burst the tyrant's chain,
        Maryland!
Virginia should not call in vain,
        Maryland!
She meets her sisters on the plain,—
"*Sic semper!*" 'tis the proud refrain
That baffles minions back amain,
        Maryland, my Maryland!

I see the blush upon thy cheek,
        Maryland!
For thou wast ever bravely meek,
        Maryland!
But lo! there surges forth a shriek
From hill to hill, from creek to creek,—
Potomac calls to Chesapeake,
        Maryland, my Maryland!

Thou wilt not yield the Vandal toll,
    Maryland!
Thou wilt not crook to his control,
    Maryland!
Better the fire upon thee roll,
Better the blade, the shot, the bowl,
Than crucifixion of the soul,
        Maryland, my Maryland!

I hear the distant thunder-hum,
    Maryland!
The Old Line's bugle, fife, and drum,
    Maryland!
She is not dead, nor deaf, nor dumb;
Huzza! she spurns the Northern scum!
She breathes! she burns! she'll come!
    she'll come!
        Maryland, my Maryland!

DIXIE
Albert Pike (1809–1891)

★ ★ ★ ★ ★ ★ ★

Southrons, hear your country call you!
Up, lest worse than death befall you!
   To arms! To arms! To arms, in Dixie!
Lo! all the beacon-fires are lighted,—
Let all hearts be now united!
   To arms! To arms! To arms, in Dixie!
      Advance the flag of Dixie!
        Hurrah! hurrah!
For Dixie's land we take our stand,
     And live or die for Dixie!
       To arms! To arms!
    And conquer peace for Dixie!
       To arms! To arms!
    And conquer peace for Dixie!

Hear the Northern thunders mutter!
Northern flags in South winds flutter!
Send them back your fierce defiance!
Stamp upon the accursed alliance!

Fear no danger! Shun no labor!
Lift up rifle, pike, and sabre!
Shoulder pressing close to shoulder,
Let the odds make each heart bolder!

How the South's great heart rejoices
At your cannons' ringing voices!
For faith betrayed, and pledges broken,
Wrongs inflicted, insults spoken.

Strong as lions, swift as eagles,
Back to their kennels hunt these beagles!
Cut the unequal bonds asunder!
Let them hence each other plunder!

Swear upon your country's altar
Never to submit or falter,
Till the spoilers are defeated,
Till the Lord's work is completed!

Halt not till our Federation
Secures among earth's powers its station!
Then at peace, and crowned with glory,
Hear your children tell the story!

If the loved ones weep in sadness,
Victory soon shall bring them gladness,—
　　　　To arms!
Exultant pride soon vanish sorrow;
Smiles chase tears away to-morrow.
　　To arms! To arms! To arms, in Dixie!
　　　Advance the flag of Dixie!
　　　　　Hurrah! hurrah!
For Dixie's land we take our stand,
　　　And live or die for Dixie!
　　　　　To arms! To arms!
　　And conquer peace for Dixie!
　　　　　To arms! To arms!
　　And conquer peace for Dixie!

SONGS
OF THE
CIVIL
WAR

The wide variety of songs from the Civil War era extends from justifiably famous tunes to verses once popularly recognized and now obscured by time.

Among the highlights of this section are "When Johnny Comes Marching Home," a rousing battle song sung by Union soldiers returning from service and the famous flag song "The Battlecry of Freedom." Samuel Hawkins Marshall Byers' "Sherman's March to the Sea," was written while Byers was a prisoner in Columbia, South Carolina, and General Sherman was said to have preferred this dramatization of his famous march over Henry Clay Work's "Marching Through Georgia."

"The Southern Marseillaise" was the rallying song of the Confederacy, and it was sung as early as 1861 by soldiers rushing to Virginia. "The Bonnie Blue Flag" was created in conjunction with South Carolina's brand new banner—a blue flag with a single white star in the center. "Volunteer Song" was written for the New Orleans Ladies' Military Fair in 1861, and sung by regiments leaving for Virginia. "We Are Coming, Father Abraham" was written in 1862, after Lincoln had asked for 300,000 new army volunteers. "They Look Like Men of War" was sung by the Ninth Regiment U.S. Colored Troops at Benedict, Maryland, during the winter of 1863–64. "Cheer, Boys, Cheer" was the inspired song of the Southern Kentucky and Tennessee Regiments. Dan Emmet's original version of "Dixie" was first sung at Dan Bryant's minstrel show in New York, just before the war began. The famous southern version of "Dixie" (by Albert Pike) appears in the "Famous Lyrics" section of this book; the northern version follows Emmet's original.

Like the poetry of the period, the songs of the Civil War range from the patriotic to the sentimental. The concluding works in this section are in the sentimental mode, from "Tenting on the Old Camp Ground" and "We Have Drunk from the Same Canteen" to "Mother Kissed Me in My Dream" and that great song of the South, "Lorena."

WHEN JOHNNY COMES MARCHING HOME

Patrick Sarsfield Gilmore

★ ★ ★ ★ ★ ★ ★

When Johnny comes marching home again,
    Hurrah! Hurrah!
We'll give him a hearty welcome then,
    Hurrah! Hurrah!
The men will cheer, the boys will shout,
The ladies they will all turn out.

Chorus—
    And we'll all feel gay,
When Johnny comes marching home.

The old church-bell will peal with joy,
    Hurrah! Hurrah!
To welcome home our darling boy,
    Hurrah! Hurrah!
The village lads and lasses say
With roses they will strew the way.

THE BATTLECRY OF FREEDOM

George Frederick Root

★ ★ ★ ★ ★ ★ ★

Yes, we'll rally round the flag, boys, we'll rally
      once again,
    Shouting the battlecry of freedom,
We will rally from the hillside, we'll gather
      from the plain,
    Shouting the battlecry of freedom.

Chorus—
    The Union forever, hurrah! boys, hurrah!
    Down with the traitor, up with the star,
    While we rally round the flag, boys,
    Rally once again,
    Shouting the battle cry of Freedom.

We are springing to the call of our
      brothers gone before,
    Shouting the battlecry of freedom.
And we'll fill the vacant ranks with a
      million freemen more,
    Shouting the battlecry of freedom.

SHERMAN'S MARCH TO THE SEA

Samuel Hawkins Marshall Byers

Our camp-fires shone bright on the mountains
   That frowned on the river below,
While we stood by our guns in the morning,
   And eagerly watched for the foe;
When a rider came out from the darkness
   That hung over mountain and tree,
And shouted: "Boys, up and be ready!
   For Sherman will march to the sea."

Then cheer upon cheer for bold Sherman
   Went up from each valley and glen,
And the bugles re-echoed the music
   That came from the lips of the men;
For we knew that the stars in our banner
   More bright in their splendor would be,
And that blessings from Northland would greet us
   When Sherman marched down to the sea.

Then forward, boys! forward to battle!
   We marched on our perilous way,
And we stormed the wild hills of Resaca—
   God bless those who fell on that day!
Then Kenesaw, dark in its glory,
   Frowned down on the flag of the free,
But the East and the West bore our standards
   And Sherman marched on to the sea.

Still onward we pressed till our banners
   Swept out from Atlanta's grim walls,

And the blood of the patriot dampened
  The soil where the traitor flag falls.
We paused not to weep for the fallen,
  Who sleep by each river and tree,
But we twined them a wreath of the laurel,
  And Sherman marched on to the sea.

Oh, proud was our army that morning,
  That stood where the pine darkly towers,
When Sherman said, "Boys, you are weary,
  But to-day fair Savannah is ours."
Then sang we a song for our chieftain,
  That echoed o'er river and lea,
And the stars in our banner shone brighter
  When Sherman marched down to the sea.

MARCHING THROUGH GEORGIA
Henry Clay Work

Bring the good old bugle, boys, we'll sing another song—
Sing it with a spirit that will start the world along—
Sing it as we used to sing it, fifty thousand strong,
While we were marching through Georgia.

Chorus—
  "Hurrah! Hurrah! we bring the jubilee,
  Hurrah! Hurrah! the flag that makes you free!"
  So we sang the chorus from Atlanta to the sea,
  While we were marching through Georgia.

How the darkeys shouted when they heard the joyful sound!
How the turkeys gobbled which our commissary found!
How the sweet potatoes even started from the ground,
While we were marching through Georgia.

THE SOUTHERN MARSEILLAISE
A. E. Blackmar

★ ★ ★ ★ ★ ★ ★

Sons of the South, awake to glory,
   A thousand voices bid you rise,
Your children, wives and grandsires hoary,
    Gaze on you now with trusting eyes,
    Gaze on you now with trusting eyes;
Your country every strong arm calling,
    To meet the hireling Northern band
    That comes to desolate the land
With fire and blood and scenes appalling,
    To arms, to arms, ye brave;
    Th' avenging sword unsheath!
March on! March on! All hearts resolved on
      victory or death.
March on! March on! All hearts resolved on
      victory or death.

Now, now, the dangerous storm is rolling,
   Which treacherous brothers madly raise,
The dogs of war let loose, are howling,
    And soon our peaceful towns may blaze,
    And soon our peaceful towns may blaze.

Shall fiends who basely plot our ruin,
 Unchecked, advance with guilty stride
 To spread destruction far and wide,
With Southron's blood their hands embruing?
 To arms, to arms, ye brave!
 Th' avenging sword unsheath!
March on! March on! All hearts resolved on
 victory or death,
March on! March on! All hearts resolved on
 victory or death.

BLUE COATS ARE OVER THE BORDER

★ ★ ★ ★ ★ ★ ★

Sung to the tune of "Blue Bonnets Are over the Border"

Kentucky's banner spreads
Its folds above our heads;
We are already famous in story.
Mount and make ready then,
Brave Duke and all his men;
Fight for our homes and Kentucky's old glory.

Chorus—
March! March! Brave Duke and all his men!
Haste, brave boys, now quickly march forward in order!
March! March! ye men of old Kentuck!
The horrid blue coats are over the border.

Morgan's men have great fame,
There is much in a name;
Ours must shine today as it ever has shone!

THE BONNIE BLUE FLAG
Harry Macarthy

★ ★ ★ ★ ★ ★ ★

We are a band of brothers, and native to the soil,
Fighting for the property we gained by honest
    toil;
And when our rights were threatened, the cry rose
    near and far,
Hurrah for the Bonnie Blue Flag that bears a
    single star!

Chorus—
Hurrah! Hurrah! for Southern Rights, hurrah!
Hurrah! for the Bonnie Blue Flag that bears a
    single star!

As long as the Union was faithful to her trust,
Like friends and like brothers we were kind, we
    were just;
But now when Northern treachery attempts our
    rights to mar,
We hoist on high the Bonnie Blue Flag that bears
    a single star.

VOLUNTEER SONG

★ ★ ★ ★ ★ ★ ★

"Go soldiers, arm you for the fight,
God shield the cause of Justice, Right;
May all return with victory crowned,
May every heart with joy abound,
May each deserve the laurel crown,
Nor one to meet his lady's frown.

"Your cause is good, 'tis honor bright,
'Tis virtue, country, home and right;
Then should you die for love of these,
We'll waft your names upon the breeze:
The waves will sing your lullaby,
Your country mourn your latest sigh."

WE'LL BE FREE IN MARYLAND
Robert E. Holtz

★ ★ ★ ★ ★ ★ ★

The boys down south in Dixie's land,
The boys down south in Dixie's land,
The boys down south in Dixie's land,
Will come and rescue Maryland.

Chorus—

If you will join the Dixie band,
Here's my heart and here's my hand,
If you will join the Dixie band;
We're fighting for a home.

We'll rally to Jeff Davis true,
Beauregard and Johnston, too,
Magruder, Price, and General Bragg,
And give three cheers for the Southern flag.

SLEEPING FOR THE FLAG
Henry Clay Work

★ ★ ★ ★ ★ ★ ★

When the boys come home in triumph, brother,
With the laurels they shall gain;
When we go to give them welcome, brother,
We shall look for you in vain.
We shall wait for your returning, brother,
You were set forever free;
For your comrades left you sleeping, brother,
Underneath a Southern tree.

Chorus—

Sleeping to waken in this weary world no more;
Sleeping for your true lov'd country, brother,
Sleeping for the flag you bore.

You who were the first on duty, brother,
When "to arms" your leader cried,—

You have left the ranks forever,
You have laid your arms aside,
From the awful scenes of battle, brother,
You were set forever free;
When your comrades left you sleeping, brother,
Underneath the Southern tree.

WE ARE COMING,
FATHER ABRAHAM

James Sloan Gibbons

★ ★ ★ ★ ★ ★

We are coming, Father Abraham, three hundred
    thousand more,
From Mississippi's winding stream and from New
    England's shore;
We leave our ploughs and workshops, our wives
    and children dear,
With hearts too full for utterance, with but a
    single tear;
We dare not look behind us, but steadfastly
    before:
We are coming, Father Abraham, three hundred
    thousand more!

Chorus—
We are coming, we are coming, our Union to
    restore:
We are coming, Father Abraham, three hundred
    thousand more,

We are coming, Father Abraham, three hundred
    thousand more.

You have called us, and we're coming, by Rich-
    mond's bloody tide
To lay us down, for Freedom's sake, our brothers'
    bones beside;
Or from foul treason's savage grasp to wrench the
    murderous blade,
And in the face of foreign foes its fragments to
    parade.
Six hundred thousand loyal men and true have
    gone before:
We are coming, Father Abraham, three hundred
    thousand more!

SONG OF THE TEXAS RANGERS
J. D. Young

★ ★ ★ ★ ★ ★ ★

Sung to the tune of "The Yellow Rose of Texas"

The morning star is paling; the camp fires flicker low;
Our steeds are madly neighing; for the bugle bids us go:
So put the foot in stirrup and shake the bridle free,
For today the Texas Rangers must cross the Tennessee.
With Wharton for our leader, we'll chase the dastard foe,
Till our horses bathe their fetlocks in the deep, blue Ohio.

'Tis joy to be a Ranger! to fight for dear Southland!
'Tis joy to follow Wharton, with his gallant, trusty band!

'Tis joy to see our Harrison plunge, like a meteor bright,
Into the thickest of the fray, and deal his deadly might.
O! who'd not be a Ranger and follow Wharton's cry!
And battle for his country, and, if needs be, die?

THEY LOOK LIKE MEN OF WAR

★ ★ ★ ★ ★ ★ ★

Hark! listen to the trumpeters,
They call for volunteers,
On Zion's bright and flowery mount—
Behold the officers!

Chorus—
They look like men,
They look like men,
They look like men of war.

THE ALABAMA
E. King and F. W. Rasier

★ ★ ★ ★ ★ ★ ★

The wind blows off yon rocky shore,
Boys, set your sails all free:
And soon the booming cannon's roar
Shall ring out merrily.
Run up your bunting, caught a-peak,

And swear, lads, to defend her:
'Gainst every foe, where'er we go,
Our motto—"No surrender."

Chorus—
Then sling the bowl, drink every soul
A toast to the *Alabama,*
Whate'er our lot, through storm or shot,
Here's success to the *Alabama.*

THE SOUTHERN SOLDIER BOY
G. W. Alexander

★ ★ ★ ★ ★ ★ ★

Sung to the tune of "The Boy with the Auburn Hair"

Bob Roebuck is my sweetheart's name,
    He's off to the wars and gone,
He's fighting for his Nannie dear,
    His sword is buckled on;
He's fighting for his own true love,
    His foes he does defy;
He is the darling of my heart,
    My Southern soldier boy.

Chorus—
Yo! ho! yo! ho! yo! ho! ho! ho! ho! ho! ho!
    He is my only joy,
He is the darling of my heart,
    My Southern soldier boy.

THE ZOUAVES
J. Howard Wainwright

★ ★ ★ ★ ★ ★ ★

Onward, Zouaves,—Ellsworth's spirit leads us;
Onward, Zouaves, for our country needs us;
Onward, Zouaves, for our banner floats o'er us;
Onward Zouaves, for the foe is before us.

Chorus—
Onward Zouaves!
Do nothing by halves:
Home to the hilt, with the bay'net, Zouaves.

MY OLD KENTUCKY HOME, GOOD NIGHT
Stephen C. Foster

★ ★ ★ ★ ★ ★ ★

The sun shines bright in the old Kentucky home;
  'Tis summer, the darkeys are gay,
The corn-top's ripe and the meadow's in the
    bloom,
  While the birds make music all the day.

The young folks roll on the little cabin floor,
  All merry, all happy and bright;
By-'n-by hard times comes a-knocking at the
    door:—
  Then my old Kentucky home, good-night!

Chorus—
  Weep no more, my lady,
  Oh! weep no more today!
  We will sing one song for the old Kentucky home,
  For the old Kentucky home, far away.

OLD FOLKS AT HOME
Stephen C. Foster

★ ★ ★ ★ ★ ★

Way down upon de Swanee Ribber,
  Far, far away,
Dere's wha my heart is turning ebber,
  Dere's wha de old folks stay.
All up and down de whole creation
  Sadly I roam,
Still longing for de old plantation,
  And for de old folks at home!

Chorus—
All de world am sad and dreary,
  Ebery where I roam;
Oh, darkeys, how my heart grows weary,
  Far from de old folks at home!

CHEER, BOYS, CHEER

Cheer, boys, cheer! no more of idle sorrow;
Courage! true hearts shall bear us on our way;
Hope points before and shows a bright tomorrow,
Let us forget the darkness of today:
Then farewell, England, much as we may love
        thee,
We'll dry the tears that we have shed before;
We'll not weep to sail in search of fortune;
Then farewell, England, farewell forevermore.

Chorus—
Then cheer, boys, cheer! for England, Mother
        England.
Cheer boys, cheer for the willing strong right
        hand;
Cheer, boys, cheer! there's wealth in honest labor;
Cheer, boys, cheer for the new and happy land.

TO CANAAN

Where are you going, soldiers,
With banner, gun and sword?
We're marching south to Canaan
To battle for the Lord.
What Captain leads your armies
Along the rebel coasts?
The mighty One of Israel,
His name is Lord of Hosts.

Chorus—
   To Canaan, to Canaan,
The Lord has led us forth,
To blow before the heathen walls
The trumpets of the North.

DIXIE
Dan Emmet

* * * * * * *

The original version

I wish I was in de land ob cotton,
Old times dar am not forgotten;
Look away, look away, look away,
    Dixie Land.
In Dixie Land whar I was born in,
Early on one frosty mornin,'
Look away, look away, look away, Dixie Land.

Chorus—
Den I wish I was in Dixie,
    Hooray! Hooray!
In Dixie Land, I'll took my stand,
To lib and die in Dixie:
Away, away, away, down South in Dixie
Away, away, away, down South in Dixie.

DIXIE
John Savage

★ ★ ★ ★ ★ ★ ★

The Union adaptation

Oh, the Starry Flag is the flag for me;
'Tis the flag of life, 'tis the flag of the free,
Then hurrah, hurrah, for the flag of the Union.
Oh, the Starry Flag is the flag for me.
'Tis the flag of life, 'tis the flag of the free.
We'll raise that starry banner, boys,
Where no power or wrath can face it;

    O'er town and field—
    The people's shield;
No treason can erase it;
    O'er all the land,
    That flag must stand,
Where the people's might shall place it.

TENTING ON THE OLD CAMP GROUND
Walter Kittridge

★ ★ ★ ★ ★ ★ ★

We're tenting tonight on the old camp ground,
    Give us a song to cheer
Our weary hearts, a song of home,
    And friends we love so dear.

Many are the hearts that are weary tonight,
　Wishing for the war to cease;
Many are the hearts that are looking for the right,
　To see the dawn of peace.
Tenting tonight, tenting tonight,
　Tenting on the old camp ground.

We've been tenting tonight on the old camp
　　ground,
　Thinking of days gone by,
Of the loved ones at home that gave us the hand,
　And the tear that said "Good-bye!"

We are tired of war on the old camp ground,
　Many are dead and gone,
Of the brave and true who've left their homes;
　Others been wounded long.

We've been fighting today on the old camp
　　ground,
　Many are lying near;
Some are dead and some are dying,
　Many are in tears.

WE HAVE DRUNK FROM THE SAME CANTEEN

Charles Graham Halpine

★ ★ ★ ★ ★ ★ ★

There are bonds of all sorts in this world of ours,
Fetters of friendship and ties of flowers,
   And true lovers' knots, I ween;
The boy and the girl are bound by a kiss,
But there's never a bond, old friend, like this:
   We have drunk from the same canteen.

Chorus—
   The same canteen, my soldier friend,
   The same canteen,
   There's never a bond, old friend, like this!
   We have drunk from the same canteen.

It was sometimes water, and sometimes milk,
Sometimes applejack, fine as silk,
   But whatever the tipple has been,
We shared it together, in bane or bliss,
And I warm to you, friend, when I think of this:
   We have drunk from the same canteen.

MOTHER KISSED ME IN MY DREAM

★ ★ ★ ★ ★ ★ ★

Lying on my dying bed
   Thro' the dark and silent night,
Praying for the coming day,
   Came a vision to my sight.
Near me stood the forms I loved,
   In the sunlight's mellow gleam:
Folding me unto her breast,
   Mother kissed me in my dream.

Comrades, tell her, when you write,
   That I did my duty well;
Say that when the battle raged,
   Fighting, in the van I fell;

Tell her, too, when on my bed
   Slowly ebbed my being's stream,
How I knew no peace until
   Mother kissed me in my dream.

GAY AND HAPPY

★ ★ ★ ★ ★ ★ ★

We're the boys that's gay and happy,
   Wheresoever we may be;

And we'll do our best to please you,
    If you will attentive be.

Chorus—
    So let the wide world wag as it will,
    We'll be gay and happy still,
    Gay and happy, gay and happy,
    We'll be gay and happy still.

We envy neither great nor wealthy,
    Poverty we ne'er despise;
Let us be contented, healthy,
    And the boon we dearly prize.

The rich have cares we little know of,
    All that glitters is not gold,
Merit's seldom made a show of,
    And true worth is rarely told.

THE GIRL I LEFT BEHIND ME
Samuel Lover

* * * * * *

The hour was sad I left the maid, a lingering
    farewell taking,
Her sighs and tears my steps delay'd, I thought
    her heart was breaking;
In hurried words her name I bless'd, I breathed
    the vows that bind me,

And to my heart in anguish press'd the girl I
    left behind me.

Then to the East we bore away, to win a name
    in story,
And there where dawns the sun of day, there
    dawns our sun of glory;
Both blazed in noon on Alma's height, where in
    the post assign'd me,
I shar'd the glory of that fight, Sweet Girl I Left
    Behind Me.

THE FADED COAT OF BLUE
J. H. McNaughton

★ ★ ★ ★ ★ ★ ★

My brave lad he sleeps in his faded coat of blue;
In a lonely grave unknown lies the heart that
    beat so true;
He sank faint and hungry among the famished
    brave,
And they laid him sad and lonely within his name-
    less grave.

Chorus—
No more the bugle calls the weary one,
Rest noble spirit, in thy grave unknown!
I'll find you and know you, among the good and
    true,
When a robe of white is giv'n for the faded coat
    of blue.

He cried, "Give me water and just a little crumb,
And my mother she will bless you through all the
    years to come;
Oh! tell my sweet sister, so gentle, good and true,
That I'll meet her up in heaven, in my faded coat
    of blue."

LORENA

The years creep slowly by, Lorena;
    The snow is on the grass again;
The sun's low down the sky, Lorena;
    The frost gleams where the flowers have been.
But the heart throbs on as warmly now
    As when the summer days were nigh;
Oh! the sun can never dip so low
    Adown affection's cloudless sky.

A hundred months have passed, Lorena,
    Since last I held that hand in mine,
And felt the pulse beat fast, Lorena,
    Though mine beat faster far than thine.
A hundred months—'twas flowery May,
    When up the hilly slope we climbed,
To watch the dying of the day
    And hear the distant church bells chime.

ONE I LEFT THERE

Soft blows the breath of morning
  In my own valley fair,
For it's there the opening roses
  With fragrance scent the air,
  With fragrance scent the air.
  And with perfume fill the air,
But the breath of one I left there
  Is sweeter far to me.

Soft fall the dews of evening
  Around our valley bowers;
And they glisten on the grass plots
  And tremble on the flowers,
  And tremble on the flowers
  Like jewels rich to see,
But the tears of one I left there
  Are richer gems to me.

O WRAP THE FLAG AROUND ME, BOYS

R. Stewart Taylor

O, wrap the flag around me, boys,
To die were far more sweet,
With Freedom's starry banner, boys,

To be my winding sheet.
In life I lov'd to see it wave,
And follow where it led,
And now my eyes grow dim, my hands
Would clasp its last bright shred.

Chorus—
Then wrap the flag around me, boys,
Yet wrap the flag around me, boys,
So wrap the flag around me, boys,
To die were far more sweet,
With Freedom's starry emblem, boys,
To be my winding sheet.

JUST BEFORE THE BATTLE, MOTHER
George Frederick Root

* * * * * * *

Just before the battle, mother,
    I am thinking most of you,
While, upon the field, we're watching,
    With the enemy in view.

Comrades brave are round me lying,
    Filled with thoughts of home and God;
For well they know that, on the morrow,
    Some will sleep beneath the sod.

Chorus—
    Farewell, mother, you may never,
    You may never, mother,
    Press me to your breast again;
    But O, you'll not forget me,
    Mother, you will not forget me
    If I'm number'd with the slain.

COVER THEM OVER
WITH BEAUTIFUL FLOWERS

E. F. Stewart

* * * * * * *

Cover them over with beautiful flow'rs,
Deck them with garlands, those brothers of ours,
Lying so silently night and day,
Sleeping the years of their manhood away,
Give them the meed they have won in the past,
Give them the honors their future forecast,
Give them the chaplets they won in the strife,
Give them the laurels they lost with their life.

Chorus—
Cover them over, yes, cover them over,
Parent, and husband, brother and lover;
Crown in your hearts those dead heroes of ours,
Cover them over with beautiful flow'rs.

LOW IN THE GROUND
THEY'RE RESTING
Collin Coe

* * * * * * *

Low in the ground they're resting,
Proudly the flag waves o'er them;
Never more 'mid wars contesting
To save the land that bore them!

Chorus—
Sleep, brave ones, rest, in hallow'd graves!
Our flag now proudly o'er you waves!
Vict'ry and fame, vict'ry and fame,
Loudly forever shall your brave deeds proclaim,
Loudly forever shall your brave deeds proclaim.

WHEN THIS CRUEL WAR IS OVER
Charles Carroll Sawyer

* * * * * * *

Dearest love, do you remember,
When we last did meet,
How you told me that you loved me,
Kneeling at my feet?
Oh, how proud you stood before me,
In your suit of blue,
When you vowed to me and country
Ever to be true.

Chorus—
Weeping, sad and lonely,
Hopes and fears how vain!
Yet praying, when this cruel war is over,
Praying that we meet again!

INDEX OF
FIRST LINES

Glory and honor and fame and everlasting laudation, 95
"Go soldiers, arm you for the fight, 211

Halt!—the march is over, 18
Hark! listen to the trumpeters, 215
Have you heard the story that gossips tell, 113

I hear again the tread of war go thundering through the land, 87
I picture her there in the quaint old room, 70
I read last night of the Grand Review, 128
I see before me now a traveling army halting, 16
"I was with Grant"—the stranger said, 48
I wish I was in de land ob cotton, 221
It was that fierce contested field when Chickamauga lay, 90

Just as the spring came laughing through the strife, 79
Just before the battle, mother, 230

Kentucky's banner spreads, 209

Lists all white and blue in the skies, 176
Look on this cast, and know the hand, 141
Low in the ground they're resting, 232
Lying on my dying bed, 225

Mine eyes have seen the glory of the coming of the Lord, 193
My brave lad he sleeps in his faded coat of blue, 227

'Neath the lances of the tropic sun, 185
Not as when some great Captain falls, 143

O Captain! my Captain! our fearful trip is done, 139
O gallant brothers of the generous South, 174
O subtle, musky, slumbrous clime, 10
O, wrap the flag around me, boys, 229

There was no union in the land, 110
This bronze doth keep the very form and mould, 140
To the brave all homage render, 81
Two armies covered hill and plain, 51

Up from the South, at break of day, 40

Victors, living, with laureled brow, 120

Was there ever message sweeter, 66
Way down upon de Swanee Ribber, 218
We are a band of brothers, and native to the soil, 210
We are coming, Father Abraham, 213
We do accept thee, heavenly Peace, 127
We're tenting tonight on the old camp ground, 222
We're the boys that's gay and happy, 225
When all the sky was wild and dark, 96
When Johnny comes marching home again, 204
When lilacs last in the dooryard bloom'd, 158
When the boys come home in triumph, brother, 212
Where are you going, soldiers, 220
Who with the soldiers was stanch danger-sharer, 38
With its cloud of skirmishers in advance, 17

Yes, we'll rally round the flag, boys, 205

X-TREME LATIN

LINGUA LATINA EXTREMA

All the Latin you need to
know for surviving
the 21st century

HENRY BEARD
HENRICUS BARBATUS

headline

First published in 2004
by Gotham Books, a division of Penguin Group (USA) Inc.

First published in Great Britain in 2004
by HEADLINE BOOK PUBLISHING

This edition first published in Great Britain in 2005
by HEADLINE BOOK PUBLISHING

1

ISBN 0 7553 1296 1

Illustrations by Valerie Baker

Designed by Viv Mullett

Typeset in Dante MT by Avon DataSet Ltd, Bidford-on-Avon, Warks
Printed and bound in Great Britain by Clays Ltd St Ives plc

Headline's policy is to use papers that are natural, renewable and recyclable
products and made from wood grown in sustainable forests. The logging and
manufacturing processes are expected to conform to the environmental
regulations of the country of origin.

HEADLINE BOOK PUBLISHING
A division of Hodder Headline
338 Euston Road
London NW1 3BH

www.headline.co.uk
www.hodderheadline.com

Contents
INDEX CAPITUM

II. INTERMEDIATE LATIN

III. ADVANCED LATIN

Author's Note

Although I did the original Latin composition for the first draft of this book, my translations have been extensively corrected, meticulously polished, and felicitously rephrased by J. Mark Sugars, Ph.D., without whose assistance I would have been in *merda profundissima* (very deep doo-doo). Thus, to the extent that the classical constructions herein are historically appropriate, grammatically accurate, and culturally apt, it is he who deserves the imposing, but tasteful, triumphal arch on the sunny side of the Forum, just below the Palatine Hill. If, however, there are any *errata ignominiosa* (cock ups), it is I and I alone who should be exiled to the remote, windswept tip of some godforsaken island inhabited by rude barbarians. (The Hamptons will do nicely.)

That said, I have to confess that even the most dedicated Latin purist inevitably succumbs to the temptation to make a cheap joke at the expense of the noble tongue of Rome's golden age, and I am no exception. Therefore, in the interests of scholarly integrity, I am compelled to concede that there is no Latin verb *'geronimo, geronimare'* meaning 'to express an intention to act boldly or rashly,' say, just prior to jumping off a bridge, and if a Roman diner wished to remark, 'I will recommend this restaurant,' *'zago, zagas, zagat'* is not the way he would have phrased it. The rest of the Augustan yadda-yadda (*'iaddo, iaddere, iaddedi, iadditum'*) is as kosher as we could make it.

Oh, all right. Yadda-yadda is actually *blatero, blaterare*. Sheesh.

Preface
PRAEFATIO
PRY-FAH-TIH-OH

It's often said that Latin is a dead language
Lingua Latina saepe dicitur mortua esse
LEEN-gwah lah-TEE-nah SIGH-pay DEE-kih-tuhr MOHR-too-ah EHS-seh

Bollocks!
Coleus!
Koh-LEE-uhs!

It's just been taking a long nap
Modum iam pridem meridiatur
MOH-duhm yahm PREE-dehm meh-ree-dih-AH-tuhr

And it's been talking a lot in its sleep
Iam diu autem multa verba facit dormiens
Yahm DIH-ooh OW-tehm MOOL-tah WEHR-bah FAH-kiht DOHR-mih-ehns

In fact, you can't get it to shut up
Re vera, non potes eam in silentium redigere
Ray WAY-rah nohn POH-tess EH-ahm ihn sih-LAYN-tih-uhm reh-DIHG-eh-reh

Look around – Latin is all over the place, like a cheap toga

Circumspice – Lingua Latina se pandit ubique tanquam toga vilis

KEER-kuhm-spih-keh – LEEN-gwah lah-TEE-nah say PAHN-diht ooh-BEE-kweh TAHN-kwaum TOH-gah WIH-liss

Lawyers use it to screw you

Iurisperiti ea utuntur ut te defraudent

Yoo-riss-peh-REE-tee EH-ah uh-TOON-tuhr uht tay deh-FROW-dehnt

Doctors use it to scare you shitless

Medici hac lingua utuntur ut alvum evacues ex metu

MEH-dih-kee hock LEEN-gwah uh-TOON-tuhr uht AHL-wuhm ay-WAH-koo-ays eks MEH-tooh

Politicians use it to hide their tracks while they rob you blind

Magistratus ea utuntur ad operienda vestigia cum te despoliant

Mah-gihs-TRAH-toohs EH-ah uh-TOON-tuhr ahd oh-pehr-ih-AYN-dah wehs-TEE-gih-ah kuhm tay deh-SPOH-lih-ahnt

Priests use it to weasel their way out when they get caught playing hide-the-sausage with the altar boys

Sacerdotes in stupro cum acolytis deprehensi ea utuntur ut se criminibus absolvant

Sah-kehr-DOH-tays ihn STOOP-roh kuhm ah-koh-LEE-teese day-preh-HAYN-see EH-ah uh-TOON-tuhr uht say krih-MIHN-ih-buhss ahb-SOHL-wahnt

Even garden supply stores use it to get you to buy
  overpriced, short-lived houseplants

**Etiam venditores rerum hortensium ea utuntur ad
  persuadendum tibi ut emas maximo pretio plantas
  vitae brevis**

*EH-tih-ahm wehn-dih-TOHR-ace RAY-ruhm hohr-TAYN-sih-
  uhm EH-ah uh-TOON-tuhr ahd pehr-swah-DAYN-duhm TIH-
  bee uht EH-mahs MAHK-sih-moh PREH-tih-oh PLAHN-tahs
  WEE-tye BREH-wihss*

The fact is, for too long these dirtbags have had a
  monopoly on this mighty tongue

**Diutius quidem haec propudia monopolio huius
  magnifici sermonis fruuntur**

*Dih-OO-tih-uhs KWIH-dehm hike proh-POOH-dih-ah moh-
  noh-POH-lih-oh HOO-eeh-uhss mahg-NIH-fih-kee sehr-MOH-
  nihss frooh-OON-tuhr*

But now, thanks to this little book, you too can tap the
  awesome power of Latin to dismay the ignorant
  multitudes

**Nunc vero, huius libelli gratia, tu quoque potentia
  reverenda linguae Latinae uti potes ad indoctum
  vulgus consternandum**

*Nuhnk WAY-roh, HOO-eeh-uhss lih-BEHL-lee GRAH-tih-ah,
  too KWOH-kweh poh-TAYN-tih-ah reh-weh-RAYN-dah
  LEEN-gwigh LAH-tih-nigh OO-tee POH-tehss ahd ihn-
  DOHK-tuhm WUHL-guhs kohn-stehr-NAHN-duhm*

And best of all, you'll be able to insult and abuse one and
all in perfect safety, using a language that everyone
respects but practically no one understands

**Atque haec est optima ratio omnium: maledicere
cunctis hominibus et contumeliam imponere satis
impune poteris verbis augustis quae cum omnes
magno aestimant, tum nemo ferme intellegit**

*AHT-kweh hike ehst OHP-tih-mah RAH-tih-oh OHM-nih-uhm:
mah-leh-DEEK-eh-reh KOONK-tees hoh-MIHN-ih-buhss eht
kohn-tuh-MAY-lih-ahm ihm-POH-neh-reh SAH-tihss ihm-
POO-neh poh-TEH-rihss WAYR-beese ow-GOOS-teese kwy
kuhm OHM-nays MAHG-noh EYE-stih-mahnt tuhm NEH-mo
FAYR-meh ihn-TEHL-leh-giht*

And as you pepper your speech with catapult-powered
put-downs, remember the immortal words of Maximus
as he signaled the attack in Pannonia:

**Itaque cum spargis orationem tuam praepotentibus
opprobriis, memento verborum immortalium quae
Maximus fecit signum dans in Pannonia:**

*Ih-TAH-kweh kuhm SPAHR-ghiss oh-rah-tih-OH-nehm TOO-
ahm prigh-poh-TAYN-tih-buhss ohp-PROH-brih eehs, meh-
MEHN-toh wayr-BOH-ruhm ihm-mohr-TAH-lih-uhm kwigh
MAHK-sih-muhss FAY-kiht SIHG-nuhm dahns ihn Pahn-
NOH-nih-ah:*

Unleash hell!
Solve lora infernis!
SOHL-weh LOH-rah ihn-FEHR-nihss!

And have a nice day!
Et futue te ipsum!
Eht FUH-too-eh tay IHP-suhm

Latin Terms in Modern English

LEGAL LATIN

Latin word or phrase	*English meaning*
in flagrante delicto	
habeas corpus	
prima facie	you're in big trouble
nolo contendere	
res ipsa loquitur	

MEDICAL LATIN

Latin word or phrase	*English meaning*
macula	
fistula	
carcinoma	you're dead
angina	
medulla oblongata	

POLITICAL LATIN

Latin word or phrase	*English meaning*
pro forma	
ex officio	
per diem	the fix is in
sine qua non	
quid pro quo	

ECCLESIASTICAL LATIN

Latin word or phrase	*English meaning*
ex cathedra	
in pectore	
urbi et orbi	the bishop is not available
in hoc signo vinces	
sic transit gloria mundi	

BOTANICAL LATIN

Latin word or phrase	*English meaning*
grandiflora	
tomentosa	leafless clump of dry
pendula	brown twigs in one
rugosa	week flat
sempervirens	

Basic Latin Pronunciation Guide

VOWELS

a   if long, as in 'bl*ah*'; if short, as in 'rub-*a*-dub'
e   if long, as in 'ol*é*'; if short as in 'f*eh*'
i   if long, as in ''*zi*ne'; if short as in 'z*i*t'
o   if long, as in 'd'*oh*'; if short as in 'n*o*t'
u   if long, as in 'd*u*de'; if short as in 'wass*u*p'

There is really no simple way to tell if a vowel is long or short, but if the word is short – one syllable – treat the vowel as short. The last syllable of verb endings are almost always short. If *a*, *i*, *o*, or *u*, come at the end of a word, they're long; if *e* comes at the end of a word, it's short. If a vowel is followed by two consonants, it's long. For other situations, pronuntia utrolibet modo! (wing it!)

DIPTHONGS

ae   as in 'Th*ai*'
au   as in '*ou*ch'
ei   as in 'h*ey*'
eu   as in 'h*ey*, y*ou*'
oe   as in 'g*oy*'
ui   as in 'pt*ui*'

CONSONANTS

b, d, f, h, I, m, n, and *p* are the same as in English. So are *k* and *z*, which are rare in Latin anyway. *j, w,* and the consonant *y* don't exist in Latin.

c, ch   always 'k.' That's a KIGH-sahr salad you ordered. You want ANN-koh-veese with that?

g, gn   always 'guh.' The Romans were fighting the GUHR-mahns, not the JUR-mahns, and when they gave the signal to attack, it was a SIHG-nuhm (trumpet blast) not a SEE-nuhm (large bowl).

i   always 'yuh.' It's thanks to YOO-lih-uhss (not JOO-lee-yuss) that we celebrate the fourth of July instead of the fourth of Quinctil.

r   you can rrroll your r's even if they'rrre the last letterrr of a worrrrd.

s   always 'sss.' The Roman fanss (not fanz) were animalss (not animalz).

t, th   always 'teh.' Teh-hey teh-rew teh-hings at eak otteh-her during teh-he nah-tih-oh-nahl (not nashunal) ant-hem (not anthum).

v   always 'w.' The wolcano that waporized Pompeii was Weh-SOO-wee-uhss.

There are no silent letters in Latin – every vowel (unless it's part of a two-syllable dipthong) and every consonant is always pronounced fully, and often separately. Of course, there are also no actual Romans around to sneer when you mess up.

I
LINGUA LATINA
TIRONIBUS

BEGINNING LATIN

A Little Story
NARRATIUNCULA

Puellae filiae agricolarum sunt
The girls are the daughters of the farmers

Puellae pulchrae sunt
The girls are pretty

Puellae nautas in via spectant
The girls see the sailors in the street

Nautae pulchri sunt
The sailors are hunks

Puellae nautas salutant
The girls say hello to the sailors

O malam fortunam! Nautae male mares sunt
Too bad! The sailors are homos

Nautae ad puellas digitos impudicos porrigunt
The sailors give the girls the finger

Puellae nautas appellant
The girls call out to the sailors

'Speramus naviculam misellam vestram ad scopulum
adlisam iri summersum'
'We hope your stupid boat hits a rock and sinks'

Puellae in forum descendere destinant et ibi
mercimonium furari
**The girls decide to go down to the mall and shoplift
some stuff**

Omnes paucis annis prosedae erunt
In a few years they will all be hookers

Latin Aptitude Test
PROBATIO LATINITATIS

(answers below – *responsa recta in ima pagina*)

I. MATH – SCIENTIA MATHEMATICA

All Gaul is divided into ___ parts
Gallia est omnis divisa in partes ___

A. many
   multas
B. good
   bonas
C. small
   parvas
D. warlike
   bellicosas
E. Capture a Gaul and torture him until he tells you
   Torque Gallum captum donec tibi respondeat

II. VERBAL – SCIENTIA VERBORUM

Arms and the man I sing, who first from the shores of
___ . . .
Arma virumque cano ___ qui primus ab oris . . .

A. Syracuse
   Syracusarum
B. Ithaca
   Ithacae
C. Albany
   Albani
D. Buffalo
   Bufali
E. Sacrifice a bullock to Jupiter so the test gets canceled
   because the teacher was struck by lightning
   *Immola Iovi iuvencum ut magistro tacto de caelo probatio
   relinquatur*

III. EXTRA CREDIT – QUAESTIO ADDITA PRAEMII GRATIA

Whatever it is, I fear the Greeks even when bearing
_____

Quidquid id est, timeo Danaos et _____ ferentes

A. shish kebabs
   carunculas veribus fixas
B. stuffed grape leaves
   folia vitis oryza farta
C. baklava
   crustula laminosa
D. the check
   syngrapham
E. Send a slave over later with the answer, and if he gets it
   wrong, lop off his ears
   *Mitte brevi postea servum qui responsum referat atque si
   erret praecide aures ei*

I., E; II, E; III, E.

Romulus and Remus Jokes
ROMULI REMIQUE IOCULARIA

ROMULUS: Why did the sacred chicken cross the Appian Way?

ROMULUS: Quem ob rem pullus sacer viam Appiam transivit?

REMUS: I do not know. Let us cut it open and see if the entrails provide an explanation for this inauspicious behaviour!

REMUS: Nescio. Eum evisceremus ut, extane ostensura sint illius infausti facti causam, comperiamus!

ROMULUS: Why do Roman firemen wear red braces?

ROMULUS: Cur gerunt siphonarii Romani retinacula rubra?

REMUS: I do not know – let us set the city ablaze and see if their trousers fall down!

REMUS: Nescio. Urbem incendamus ut, sintne delapsurae bracae eorum, comperiamus!

ROMULUS: Why did the Helvetian moron throw the water clock out the window?

ROMULUS: Quare iecit caudex Helvetius clepsydram de fenestra?

REMUS: I do not know, but I feel certain that after ten years chained to an oar as a galley slave he will be eager to reveal the reason for his rash act!

REMUS: Nescio; pro certo tamen habeo istum, decem annos vinctum in servitio ad remum intra navem longam, cupidum futurum revelare rationem sui temerarii facti!

The Legion of Superheroes
LEGIO HEROUM MAXIMORUM

Faster than a speeding chariot . . .
Celerior quam currus festinans . . .

More powerful than a Carthaginian war-elephant . . .
Valentior quam elephas bellicus Punicus . . .

Able to conjugate irregular verbs without making a single mistake . . .
Potis anomala verba sine lapsu declinare . . .

It's Ro-Man!
Romanus est!

T-shirt Slogans
TITULI TUNICALES

CARPE NAREM
Pick your nose

CAPE SOMNUM
Catch some 'z's'

CAPIAMUS CEREVISIAM
Let's grab a beer

CAVE LABOREM
Beware of work

MORANS FAC PAUSAM UT SEDES BIROTARUM
   OLFACIAS
Take time to stop and smell the bicycle seats

PUTEO ERGO SUM
I stink, therefore I am

VENI, VIDI, VOMUI
I came, I saw, I blew lunch

SOLVE LORA INFERNIS
Unleash hell

OSTENDE MIHI PECUNIAM
Show me the money

PARENTES MEI DIMIDIUM EUROPAE DESPOLIA
   VERUNT. EGO TAMEN NIL ACCEPI PRAETER
   HANC TUNICULAM MISELLAM
**My parents plundered half of Europe and all I got was
this stupid T-shirt**

ABES ETIAM A CONSILIO INSULTANDI MIHI NISI
   LATINE LOQUI SCIAS
Don't even think of dissing me unless you speak Latin

ILLUC IVI, ILLUD FECI
Been there, done that

Bumper Stickers
TITULI CURRULES

I'd rather be pillaging
Malim praedari

I'm dumb and I vote
Hebes sum et suffragia fero

My child can beat the crap out of your wimpy honor
student
**Filius meus puerum tuum studiosum laureatum
mollem deverberare potest**

Thank you for not thanking me for not smoking
**Tibi gratias ago quod mihi gratias non agis quod
fumum non comedo**

Visualize world conquest
Habe ante oculos devictionem mundi

Keep honking – I'm reloading
Perge cornu canere – sclopetum repleo

Horn broken – watch for finger
Buccina fracta – exspecta signum digiti impudici

Barbarian on board
Barbarus in curru

Proud of our brutal police
Vigilitus nostris crudelibus gloriantes

Stop the aqueduct, save the unicorns
Sistite constructionem aquaeductus ut conservetis unicornes

I brake for lunch
Frenos inhibere soleo pransurus

Don't blame me – I voted for Miss Piggy
Nolite me culpare – Suffragatus sum Erae Porcellae

Jesus loves you – everyone else thinks you're an asshole
Te amat Iesus – ceteri te putant irrumatorem

If you can read this, I lost my trailer
Si hoc potes legere, traheam meam amisi

Reality TV
SPECTACULA TELEVISORIA VERI SIMILIA

Celebrity Shark Attack
Impetus Pistricum in Insignes

Supermodel Food Fight
Pulcherrimae Inter Se Luctantes Edulibus

Beach Babe Lapdance Showdown
Certamen Ultimum Saltandi Nympharum Litoralium in Genibus Virorum

Blow Job Island
Insula Fellatoria

Nationwide Red Alert Hot Bod Strip Search
Inquisitio Summa Cum Vigilantia Per Omnes Nationis Partes Diffusa Corporum Formosiorum Nudatorum

Meet the Organ Donors
Salvete, O Daturi Membra Post Mortem

Baby-sitters from Hell Bring Home Animals that Kill for Fun
Nutriculae Infernales in Domos Adducunt Feras Quae ad Delicias Interficiunt

Big Fat Slobs Eat Shit for Cash
Helluones Squalidi Merdam Pro Nummis Comedunt

Who Wants to Marry a Rich Old Fart with a Terminal
Disease?
Quis Vult Nubere Peditori Capulari Diviti?

Hardball Talk Shows
DISCEPTATIONES TUMULTUOSAE

That's a load of bull, and you know it!
Merae fabulae sunt, et eas esse tales scis!

You wouldn't know a fact if one hit you on the head!
Rem veram non cognoscas etiamsi frontem tibi feriat!

You're a liberal stooge!
Pedisequus parasiticus es popularium!

You're a right-wing moron!
Stipator stultus es optimatum!

See you next week!
Vos revisemus post septimanam!

Ultimate Sports
LUDI EXTRAORDINARII

Bass-fishing – Piscatus Percarum

Let me guess – you have to drink the beer to make room
in the ice chest for all the fish you catch
**Ut coniecturam faciam – necesse est tibi bibere
cerevisiam ut locum in cista glaciei des piscibus captis**

It's a keeper!
Licet mihi hunc retinere!

Stock car racing – Certamen Curruum Generalium

When are they going to start running into each other and
blowing up?
**Quando inter se collidentes incipient in flammas
dirumpi?**

Pit stop!
Statio restaurativa!

Wrestling – Luctatus

Something tells me that the mean-looking bearded guy dressed up like the Ayatollah is no match for the wily Captain America

Suspicor illum truculentum barbatum ritu archierei Persici vestitum non esse comparem Centurioni Americano vafro

Smashmouth! Smackdown!
Ictus in os! Prostratio!

Bungee jumping – Saltus de Ponte

How dumb would you have to be to jump off a bridge with a rope tied to your foot?
Quam vecors sit is qui de ponte saliat pedibus funiculo ligatis?

Geronimo!
Geronimo, geronimare!

Snowboarding – Super Nivem Labi

Hey dude, let's head to the halfpipe, catch some major air, and stick some tricks!
Heus, laute, contendamus ad canalem nivalem ut aerem oppido capientes nonnullas technas exsequamur!

Super rad! I'm stoked!
Maxime radicitus! Flagro!

The Olympics – Olympia

I'll vote for the Greek in the wrestling if you vote for the
 Roman in the chariot race
**Graeco palmam dabo in certamine luctandi si Romano
 palmam dabis in certamine quadrigarum**

Deal!
Fiat haec pactio!

Trash Talk in the Colosseum
CONTUMELIA IN AMPHITHEATRO FLAVIO

You want a part of me? Bring it on!
Visne partem mei capere? Comminus agamus!

Are you dissing me?
Insultasne tu miki?

You're yesterday's news
In actis diurnis iamdudum es celebratus

You're toast
Mox corvos pasces

You don't know your ass from a catacomb
Non possis distinguere tuum podicem a Puticulis

Your mother is so fat, when she's in town, Rome has eight hills
Mater tua tam obesa est ut cum Romae est, urbs habet octo colles

Your mother is so ugly, when the gods turned her into a pig, she thought her prayers had been answered
Mater tua tam turpis est ut cum di eam mutaverint in porcam, suas preces putaverit eos audivisse

Your mother is so stupid, when she found a coin with
   Caesar's name on it, she tried to return it to him
**Mater tua tam stulta est ut cum invenerit nummum
   ferentem nomen Caesaris, huic eum restituere conata
   sit**

Go ahead, punk – make my day
Age, catamite – fac mihi hunc diem felicissimum

Spring Break
FERIAE VERNALES

Road trip!
Iter faciamus!

Let's party hearty!
Pergraecemur!

Wet T-shirt contest!
Certamen inter mammosas tunicis madefactis vestitas!

Go ahead, ask for proof of age. See, I've got a Latin ID.
  I'm 2,000 years old.
**Age, scrutare chartam identitatis meam. Ecce, est mihi
  syngraphus Latinus. Duo milia annorum sum natus.**

I'm wasted!
Crapulentus sum!

I'm going to throw up!
Vomiturus sum!

Country Music Favourites
MUSICA RUSTICA
FAVORABILISSIMA

Si Telephonium Non Tintinnat, Ego Voco
If Your Phone Doesn't Ring, It's Me

Causam Tibi Dabo Bibendi
I'll Give You Something to Drink About

Quomodo Una Nocte Facta Tam Turpis Es?
How Did You Get So Ugly Overnight?

Si Dies Hodiernus Esset Piscis, Reicerem
If Today Was a Fish I'd Throw it Back

Mater Cape Malleum, Musca Sedet in Capite Patris
Mother Get the Hammer, There's a Fly on Papa's Head

Si Me Deseras, Liceatne Mihi Te Comitari?
If You Leave Me, Can I Come Too?

Quomodo Te Desiderare Potero Si Non Discesseris?
How Can I Miss You If You Won't Go Away?

Per Anulum Illa Trusit Digitum Medicinalem, Ac Ostendit
Mihi Digitum Medium
She Got the Ring, and I Got the Finger

Tu Causa Es Cur Liberi Nostri Tam Turpiculi Sint
You're the Reason Our Kids Are So Ugly

Sine Te Tam Miser Sum Ut Videaris Etiamnunc Adesse
**I'm So Miserable Without You It's Like Having You
Here**

Caput Dolet, Pedes Fetent, Iesum Non Amo
My Head Hurts, My Feet Stink, and I Don't Love Jesus

Chilling Out
SERMO OTIOSORUM

Wassup?
Quagis?

Nothin', watching the game
Nihil ago, ludos specto

True, true
Vero, vero

It's off the hook
Ab unco remotumst

Talk to the hand, the face don't understand
Adloquere manum, facies nescit quid velis

Black togas are cool
Togae atrae lepidae sunt

Want to see my sword collection?
Vin' aspicere collectum gladiorum meum?

I'm thinking of taking a catapult into the school
cafeteria . . .
Cogito ferre catapultam in cenationem scholae . . .

Graffiti
INSCRIPTIONES LATRINALES

Make love, not war – hell, get married, do both
Suscipite amorem, non bellum – eheu, iuncti matrimonio, suscipite utrumque

Procrastinate now
Procrastina rem nunc

Flush twice, it's a long way to Texas
Evacua cratera latrinalem bis, Texas procul est

If it has tits, tyres, or testicles, it's nothing but trouble
Mammeatae, rotalia, testiculati, omni modo molesta sunt

Gods are dead
Di mortui sunt

Beauty is in the eye of the beer-holder
Cervesia pota, pulchritudo cernitur

Yankee, go home – and take me with you
Americani, redite domum – ducentes me vobiscum

If we aren't supposed to eat animals, why are they made
of meat?
**Si quidem animalia nobis edenda non sunt, quare
constant ex carne?**

There are three kinds of people: those who can count,
and those who can't
**Sunt genera tria hominum: illi qui numerare possunt,
et illi qui non possunt**

It *is* as bad as you think, and they *are* out to get you
**Res tam malae sunt quam putas, et inimici re vera te
persequuntur**

Why don't psychics ever win the lottery?
**In sortitionibus donativis, cur numquam praemia
consequuntur sortilegi?**

Aunt Em: Hate you, Hate Kansas, Taking the dog –
Dorothy
**Amita Aemilia: Te Kansiamque odi, Canem mecum
abduco – Dorothea**

If walking is so good for you, why does my mailman look
like Jabba the Hut?
**Si quidem pedibus ire tam salubre corpori est, cur
similis est noster tabellarius forma illi Iabbae Hutico?**

Kill Barney
**Interfice Arcturulum, istum mimum personatum
portentosum purpureum palaeozoicum**

Road Rage
IRA IN VIA

Where did you learn to drive – fleeing from Huns?
Ubi didicisti gubernare currum? In fuga ab Hunnis?

That's it, numbnuts. Pull out in front of me, then slow
down when you get to the light.
**Euge, enervate eunuche! Ingredere in orbitam meam
prae me, tum reprime cursum cum biviali lucernae
approprinquas.**
Now speed up when I try to pass you, and as I go by, give
me the finger
**Nunc, accelera cum conor te praeterire, mihique
praetereunti ostende digitum impudicum**

Okay, tailgater – time for a brake check
Em, ichneumon – tempus est sufflamina temptare

Big car, little dick
Currus magnus, mentula minuscula

You know what S.U.V.s and hemorrhoids have in
common? Every asshole has one.
**Scisne quid commune superlativa urbana vehicula cum
haemorrhoidis habeant? Est unum ex his utrisque
malis cuique pathico.**

Lady, if you're going to sit there all day yakking on your mobile, why don't you stick a steering wheel on your living room wall and just stay home?

Muliercula, si vis ibi sedens garrire totum diem in Nokiam tuam, quidni rotam adfigens gubernalem ad murum conclavis domi maneas?

What are you saving those pretty little turn signals for – Christmas?

Quod ad tempus reservas ista lumina pulchella praemonitoria – ad Saturnalia?

No, Mr Busybody, I am not handicapped, but you will be if you don't move your nosy butt out of that parking place, pronto

Minime, ardelio, nullo modo debilis sum, sed fies tu quidem, si clunes tuas curiosas non removeris protinam ab illa statione

Don't clamp my car!

Noli caligam in rotam currus mei adfigere!

I am too allowed in the car pool lane! See, I'm not alone. I suffer from multiple personality disorder.

Certe mihi licet vehi in orbita seposita curribus repletis. Ecce, non solus sum. Legio mihi nomen est, quia multi sumus.

There are three of us here. I want to drive! No, it's my turn! Not fair, what about me? Me me me!

Adsunt tres. Volo gubernare! Immo, ordo memet vocat! Iniquum est! Quid de me? Me me me!

Does that Breathalyzer have a Latin setting?

**Potestne illa machina pneumatodocimastica ad linguam
Latinam accommodari?**

I have Vatican diplomatic immunity. If you give me a
ticket, you're going to end up cooling your heels in The
Hague in a jail cell full of Yugoslavian war criminals.

**Sedes Romana Sacra mihi diplomaticam immunitatem
tribuit. Si me vocaveris in ius, aetatem tuam deges
Hagae Comitis, conditus in carcerem refertum
Iugoslavorum condemnatorum de bellum contra ius
gentium gerendo.**

Air Rage
IRA IN AËRE

Do you have nail-clipper-sniffing dogs?
Habetisne canes quae forficulas unguales olfacere possunt?

I think that guy with a napkin on his noggin has a catapult
  in his shoe
**Credo illum mantelium in capite gerentem occultavisse
  catapultam in caliga**

Hey, pal, is that carry-on luggage or did you just sack
  Carthage?
**Heia, amice, utrum illae sunt sarcinae tuae, an modo
  Carthaginem despoliasti?**

Say, miss, didn't you used to work for Con Air?
**Dic mihi, domnicella, nonne te conducebat aëria classis
  quae condemnatos transportabat?**

You know, even galley slaves were served meals
Nempe cibus dabatur etiam servis navalibus

If there's an accident, I'm going to charge people to use
  this exit
**Si de caelo cadere incipiamus, vectores pretium pro usu
  huius exitus poscam**

Warning Labels
SCHEDAE MONITORIAE

Your nose may fall off
Fieri potest ut nasus tuus decidat

You may develop hot-dog fingers
Fieri potest ut digiti tui formam tomaculorum sumant

Your head may explode
Fieri potest ut caput tuum displodatur

Your brain may turn to mush
Fieri potest ut cerebrum tuum liquefiat

You may start babbling in Latin
Fieri potest ut Latine blaterare incipias

II
LINGUA LATINA
MEDIA

INTERMEDIATE LATIN

Caesar's PowerPoint Presentation

CAESAR TIBI PROPOSITA MAXIMI MOMENTI PRAEFERT

I

Argumentum	*Topic*
Gallia, terra in partes tres divisa	Gaul, a country with three parts
*Cisalpina	*Northern Italy
*Transalpina	*France
*Oblitus sum tertiae	*I forget

II

Consilium	*Plan*
*Visere	*Make a visit
*Videre	*Have a look-see
*Vincere	*Take it over

III

Sequelae	*Follow-up*
*De bello stultum librum scribam	*Write a stupid book about it
*A nonnullis irrumatoribus occidar in Foro	*Get assassinated in the forum by a bunch of assholes
*Acetaria et mensis accipient a me nomina	*Salad and month get named after me

IV

Conclusio	*Conclusions*
*Faciam ut animus meus scrutetur	*Get head examined
*Quid illa femella Cleopatra?	*What about that Cleopatra dame?

Top 10 Reasons to Live in the Time of the Caesars

DECEM OPTIMAE RATIONUM CUR IN AEVO CAESARUM VIVERE IUCUNDIUS ESSET

X. Calculus won't be invented for another fifteen hundred years
Calculus differentialis non invenietur intra mille quingentos annorum

IX. When you're late on a rainy day, you can always blame the sundial
Si sub Iove pluvioso serius advenias, tu culpare semper potes horologium solare

VIII. If you piss off one god, you've still got 600 left
Si deum irrites unum, sescenti tibi iam supersint

VII. Actors are treated like dirt
Histriones foede tractantur

VI. Athletes who complain about their pay end up in an urn
Athletae qui queruntur de mercedibus mox in urnas funduntur

V. Scumbags who get the death penalty think they got off light
Scelesti mortis damnati se leviores poenas pensuros reuntur

IV. The likeliest place to find some pushy Christian preacher is inside a lion
Veri simillimum est, locum in quo praedicatorem Christianum protervum invenies, ventrem leoninum esse

III. The French are an ignorant bunch of servile peasants living in smelly huts, and the Germans are getting their asses kicked
Gens Gallorum inerudita servilis agrestis est, in tuguriis foetidis habitans, et Germani vapulant

II. A healthy diet consists of waiting to see if the food taster dies before having anything to eat
Diaeta salubris est, antequam aliquid cenes, observare an moriatur praegustator

I. Everyone is always dressed for a toga party
Omnès amiciuntur semper togis quasi convivium agitaturi

That Old-Time Religion
ILLA RELIGIO PRISCA

Actually, I'm a born-again pagan
Re vera, cultor denuo renatus deorum Romanorum antiquorum sum

I get to worship whomever I like, including SpongeBob SquarePants
Licet mihi venerari pro deo quemlibet, etiam SpongoRobertum QuadratoBracatum

I always ask myself, What would Julius Caesar do?
Me semper rogo, Quid faceret Iulius Caesar?

No, as far as miracles go, this 'J.C.' never raised the dead, but he certainly lowered a lot of the living
Immo, si de miraculis agitur, ille 'I Ce' nullos mortuos ad vitam revocavit, sed tamen multos vivos ad mortem sane misit

We're having a prayer breakfast down at the rifle range
Ientabimus, precatione facta, in campo manuballistulario

I am a firm believer in tough hate
Mihi persuasum est odisse acerbe

Do unto others, but do it first
Fac hominibus aliis, atqui fac prius

Blessed are the poor, because they leave so much more
    money for the rest of us
**Beati pauperes, quoniam tanto plus pecuniae nobis
    reliquis relinquunt**

Blessed are the meek, because we can cut in front of them
    in queues
**Beati mites, quoniam istis in ordine stantibus
    anteponere nosmet ipsos possumus**

If someone smites you on the cheek, turn the other cheek
    and see what kind of a smiter he is with a bloody stump
**Si quis te percusserit in dexteram maxillam tuam,
    praebe illi alteram ut possis cognoscere quam fortiter
    percussurus sit bracchio truncato cruento**

Love thy neighbors, and to show you really mean it, send
    50,000 heavily armed soldiers to knock on their door
    and ask in the nicest possible way if they'd like to join
    your empire
**Dilige proximos tuos, utque illis ostendas te re vera
    diligere, mitte decem legiones quae ianuas pulsent et
    quam dulcissime ab illis quaerant, num velint in
    tuum imperium recipi**

The theory of evolution is baloney. Everyone knows the
    whole universe came out of Saturn's nostrils
**Theoria Darwiniana evolutionis specierum absurda est.
    Constat inter omnes universitatem rerum ab naribus
    Saturni venisse**

Of course I can speak in tongues, but I prefer Latin

Sane loqui variis linguis possum sicut Apostoli die Pentecostes, sed malo Latine loqui

Let's say grace: O gods, thank you for permitting us to gobble this food the way Caesar gobbled up half of Europe. Amen.

Precemur. O di, gratias vobis agimus, quod nos sinitis hunc cibum sic devorare quo modo C. Iulius Caesar dimidiam partem Europae devoravit. Finis.

Mob Banter
CAVILLATIO SODALIUM

It fell off the back of a truck, capeesh?
**De extremo plaustro excidit; comprehendisne mente
quod dico?**

You got a problem with that, paysan?
Num de hoc dubitas, compagane?

Whatsamatter you?
Quid te sollicitat?

Fuhgeddaboutit
Eice id ex animo

Geddouttahere
Noli mecum nugari

God forbid, a piano should fall on your head
Dii prohibeant ne clavicinium in caput tuum delabatur

New Age Discourse
SERMO NEOMYSTICUS

Meditate on this, pal
Meditare de hoc, amice

Do you know the yoga position where you put your head
between your legs and kiss your ass goodbye?
**Scisne schema gymnosophisticum per quod, capite
inter femora flexo, iubentur basio valere clunes?**

Did a dish of potpourri just catch fire, or did someone
light up a joint?
**Utrum patella florum siccatorum ignem modo
concepit, an aliquis accendit sarcinulam cannabis?**

Man, that shit is potent – I am like totally in the
subjunctive
**Mehercle, illa materia tam valida est ut funditus in
modo subiunctivo sim**

I've got the munchies! Pizza pizza!
Esurio! Libum Neapolitanum!

Hollywood Latin
SERMO LATINUS ACUIFOLIIS

I love it, I love it, I love it!
Id amo, id amo, id amo!

Make the mother the father, change the cat to a dog, and
lose the kid with cancer
**Muta matrem in patrem, converte felem in canem,
amitte puerum cancerosum**

And replace all the love scenes with car chases and set it in
the Hamptons instead of the Civil War
**Substitue autem persecutiones curriles pro episodiis
eroticis, et conloca dramatis actionem in Hamtunis in
vicem temporis Belli Civilis Americani**

Wait, the girl in the copy room hated it!
Siste, puella in scriptorio xerographico fabulam oderat!

I'm putting it in turnaround
Hoc scriptum in purgatorium committo

Pasadena
Praetermitto

You'll never eat lunch in this town again
Numquam in hoc oppido prandebis iterum

Sushi Bar Chitchat

SERMO IN TABERNA IAPONICA PULPAMENTORUM INCOCTORUM MARINORUM

No mackerel, no eel, and no slab of cold egg crud
**Mihi nullus scomber, nulla anguilla, nullum frustum
ovorum frictorum frigidorum**

When I snap apart the chopsticks, do I make a wish?
**Estne mos homini findenti virgulas prehensorias
aliquod optatum declarare?**

What's the deal with the little strip of green plastic with
the fringe on top?
**Quapropter in catillum poni solet illa taeniola plastica
viridis fimbrata?**

More tuna, please, and another California roll
**Da mihi plus de thunno, sodes, et alterum volumen
Californicum**

How do you get the little piece of fish to stick to the rice
ball?
**Quo modo cogitur segmentulum piscis globo oryzae
adhaerere?**

Are those knives as sharp as they look?
Suntne illi cultri tam acuti quam esse videntur?

You guys make great cars!
Vos vehicula praestantia fabricamini!

Sorry about those atom bombs!
Me paenitet illorum pyrobolorum atomicorum!

Thank you very much!
Vobis plurimas gratias ago!

Computer Language
SERMO LATINUS
COMPUTATORIUS

Download the goddamn file, you bug-ridden piece of shit
**Assume plicam damnatam, o tu moles muscaria
muscerdarum**

If you freeze one more time, you're going straight to the
landfill
**Si denuo congeles, confestim ibis in fossam
purgamentorum**

Yeah? Well I've got an error message for you, fuckhead –
you're about to be shut down improperly with a
sledgehammer
**Sicine? Nunc age, tibi nuntium erroris habeo, stuprator
– mox improprie sopieris malleolo**

Car Talk
DISCEPTATIO DE CURRIBUS

It's a hunk of junk!
Acervus inutilium est!

That car is so ugly, you'd have to put a pork chop on the
backseat to get the dog to ride in it
**Iste currus tam turpis est ut necesse tibi sit ponere
offam porcinam in sede postrema ut persuadeas cani
ut vehatur eo**

You deserve a smack for buying it!
Eum tam imprudenter comparando meruisti alapam!

If the rattle gets too bad, wear earplugs
Nimium si strepat, indue operimenta tuis auribus

Of course you think you can repair it – you're a moron!
Scilicet putas te currum reficere posse – stipes es!

Whatever it is, it's going to cost you five hundred bucks, if
that's what it is
**Quodcumque est, Ioachimicis tibi quingentis constabit,
siquidem est, quod esse creditur**

Try putting it in neutral and pushing it off a cliff
**Vide quid eventurum sit si, dinexo ingranagio, currum
e scopulo pepuleris**

Keep in mind, people in the rearview mirror are even
stupider than they appear
**Tene memoria, viatores conspectos in speculo
retrospicienti stultiores esse quam videntur**

And remember, don't drive like my brother!
Et memento, noli agere currum ut frater meus!

B.S.
BUBULUM STERCUS

A coyote whose habitat was destroyed by urban sprawl ate my homework

Suo tractu operto suburbio extenso, canis latrans domicilium meum ingressus praescriptum domesticum mihi devoravit

Due to global warming, my homework spontaneously combusted

Orbe terrarum nimium calefacto combustione hydrogonanthracum, pensum meum domesticum sua sponte flammam concepit

My homework was seized as evidence by mistake by CIA agents in a drug bust at the wrong address

In domum meam perperam incurrentes, vigiles qui exsequuntur usum medicamentorum illicitorum nimis studiosi pensum domesticum pro testimonio iniuste abstulerunt

My homework was forcibly recycled by eco-terrorists

Praescriptum meum domesticum per vim in fibras redactum est a sodalitate quae terrore pro Terra utitur

My homework contracted mad homework disease and
   had to be destroyed

**Necesse erat pensum domesticum meum, quod incidit
   in rabiem pensi deleri**

Strict zoning codes enacted by the town board make it
   illegal for me to work at home

**Praescriptis severis de aedificiorum usu decretis a
   decurionibus municipalibus, mihi non licet operari
   domi**

Because of a lack of international standards, the Supreme
   Court ruled 5–4 that I had to stop doing my homework
   immediately

**Normis civitati universae deficientibus, quinque ex
   iudicibus Tribunalis Supremi decreverunt, quattuor
   negantibus, ut pensum statim deponerem**

Small Talk During a Colonoscopy
COLLOCUTIO INTER COLONOSCOPIAM

Now I know how a Muppet feels
Nunc novi quid Manipupa sentiat

Any sign of the trapped miners?
Conspicisne metallicos sepultos?

Are you there yet? Are you there yet? Are you there yet?
Advenistine? Advenistine? Advenistine?

Could you provide me with an affidavit stating that my
head is not, in fact, up there?
**Potesne mihi testimonium impertire adfirmans caput
meum reapse non infixum esse podici?**

Medical Confab
CONFABULATIO CUM MEDICO

I'm afraid I have some bad news, doc
Vereor ne tristem tibi nuntium adferam, medice

I've noticed you have no concept of time – I've been
  waiting for over an hour
**Animadverti te nullam notionem temporis habere –
  nam plus quam unam horam tibi praestolatus sum**

Your handwriting on prescriptions is totally illegible and
  shows signs of dementia
**Chirographum tuum quasi demens in
  medicamentorum praescriptis nemo legere potest**

Your manner is oddly distracted
Te geris mirum in modum neglegenter

You have an extremely strange sense of humour
Inusitatissima iocaris

Your fees are insane
Mercedes tuae insanae sunt

I think you have a brain tumour
Puto te tuber in cerebro alere

I'll come by again in a year and see how you're doing
Reveniam ad annum ut cognoscam de valetudine tua

Hang in there!
Perfer et obdura!

Homeland Security
SALUS PATRIAE

I'd open these bills, but I'm afraid they may contain anthrax
**Has epistulas debitorum solutionem poscentes
aperirem, sed metuo ne bacilli anthracis insint**

The bad news is, the Martians have landed and, boy, are
they mean; the good news is they hate Arabs and they
piss gasoline
**Tristis nuntio Martios descendisse et, eheu, truculentos
esse, sed laetus nuntio illos odisse Arabes oleumque
octanum meiere**

If you don't give me this putt, the terrorists win
Nisi mihi hunc puteolum concedis, phobistae vincunt

If I can't get a decent table at a top restaurant on short
notice, the terrorists have won
**Nisi mensam opimam in popina optima extemplo
accumbere possum, phobistae vicerunt**

If you won't sleep with me, the terrorists will have won
Nisi mecum concubueris, phobistae vicerint

Get out the duct tape – I'm about to fart!
Effer fasciam adhaesivam – mox pedam!

Useful Phrases for Barbarian Evildoers
LOCUTIONES UTILES MALEFACTORIBUS BARBARIS

I surrender! Please do not fire your catapult!
Me dedo! Quaeso, noli iacere tela ballista!

There is no anti-Roman sentiment here!
Hic nemo est quin Romam amet!

We love your big chariots, fast food, and violent culture!
Amamus vestras currus immanes, cibum festinanter paratum, et cultum saevum!

We hate our wicked and corrupt leaders!
Odimus duces nostros improbos pravosque!

We welcome you as liberators, not conquerors!
Vos non victores, sed liberatores salutamus!

We never liked that dirty old city – it's so much nicer as rubble!
Istam urbem squalidam senescentem numquam dileximus – confracta, multo magis nobis placet!

If you see anything you like, don't hesitate to take it!
Si quid videtis quo delectamini, agite, capite sine mora!

We'd much rather be ruled by a distant emperor, even if he's a nitwit!

Multo malimus ab imperatore remoto regi, etiamsi frutex sit!

We'll be sure to let you know if any Huns come this way!

Curabimus ut sciatis num ulli Hunni appropinquent hac via!

Have a really nice epoch!

Sit vobis aetas felicissima!

Game Boy Chatter
HORTAMINA PUERORUM LUDENTIUM ENCHIRIDIIS LUSORIIS

Taste laser death, alien insect scum!

Oppetite mortem lumine amplificato stimulata emissione radiorum, cimices extraterrestriales foedi!

Eat hot lead, Nazi zombie robot commandos!

Vescimini glandibus plumbi candentis, velites nationalisticosocialistici cadaverosi automatarii!

Feel the keen edge of the sword of doom, no-good, stinking, corpse-eating tomb-ghouls!

Sentite aciem acrem ensis mortiferi, o larvae putidae, o bustirapi nefandi!

I am going to programme a simulation of the Roman Empire and rule it unjustly, cruelly, and incompetently!

Mihi est in animo programmare simulationem imperii Romani quam iniuste, atrociter, imperite regam!

Tax the poor!

Impone vectigalia pauperibus!

Bribe the senators!

Corrumpe pecunia senatores!

Rig the elections!
Falle comitia!

Screw minorities!
Defrauda nationes minores in tua civitate!

Pack the courts with obedient dunces!
Stipa basilicas stipitibus obsequentibus!

Arrest protestors on trumped-up charges!
Infer commenta crimina seditiosis apprehensis!

Invade other countries pretty much at random!
Infer forte temere bellum aliis gentibus!

What could possibly go wrong?
Quid nobis infeliciter fieri potest?

Modern Vatican Latin
SERMO LATINUS HODIERNUS IN VATICANO

My patron saint, Miranda, appeared to me in a vision and
told me to remain silent
**Patrona mea, Sancta Miranda, apparens mihi somnio
me iussit tacere**

Whom are you going to believe, me or some snot-nosed
little boy, no matter how cute?
**Utri vos convenit credere? Mihi, an nescio cui puero
parvulo muculento, quamlibet pulchellus sit?**

Look, these legal fees are putting quite a dent in the old
collection plate
**En, mercedes iurisperitorum discum eleemosynarium
vero vacuefaciunt**

What if I say one million Our Fathers and a couple
hundred thousand Hail Marys and we just call it even?
**Si Orationum Dominicarum decies centena milia
recitabo, Salutationumque Beatae Mariae bis vel ter
ducena milia, eritne satis?**

On the advice of counsel, I have decided to testify in Latin
**Iurisconsultus mihi suasit ut testimonium dicerem
Latine**

The devil made me do it!
Diabolus me coegit peccare!

Learned Latin for Lovers
SERMO LATINUS DOCTUS AMATORIBUS

I'm only repeating a query that dates back to the
Chaldeans, but may I ask, what is your sign?
**Si modo licet mihi te rogare idem quod antiqui
Chaldaei suas puellas rogare solebant – quo signo
nata es?**

I think it was Pliny the Elder – or was it Pliny the
Younger? – who first pioneered the concept of self-
introduction by way of the purchase of a libation, and it
is really in homage to him that I am moved to offer to
buy you a drink
**Credo Gaium Plinium Secundum Maiorem – aut Gaium
Plinium Caecilium Secundum Minorem – instituisse
ut vir, qui se notiorem puellae facere vellet, ei aliquid
liquoris Lyaei compararet; itaque in
commemorationem illius iuvat potiunculam tibi
praebere**

Cicero phrased it best, and I am merely quoting the
master when I am driven to remark, 'Nice tits.'
**Hoc Marcus Tullius optime verbis expressit, neque
profero alia quam ipsissima verba optimi omnium
oratorum cum adsevero te venustas habere mammas**

In the deathless words of the great philosopher-emperor
 Marcus Aurelius, of course I will respect you in the
 morning

**Si me decet immortalia verba usurpare Marci Aurelii,
 imperatoris illustris philosophici, certe apud me in
 honore eris, cras mane**

Just as Aeneas inquired of Dido in Book Four of the
 Aeneid after stating his desire to install his obelisk in her
 temple of love, your place or mine?

**A te quaeso, sicut in Aeneidos libro quarto Aeneas,
 elocutus desiderium erigendi suum obeliscum in
 templo Venereo Didonis, ab ea quaesivit, tuae domi
 an meae?**

Classical Kiss-offs
VALEDICTIONES ANTIQUAE

Kiss my basilisk
Basia basiliscum meum

Bite my zither
Morde citharam meam

Lick my licorice stick
Linge bacillum glycyrrhizae meum

Suck my aqueduct
Suge meum aquaeductum

Tune my lap trumpet
Tempera tubam quam in sinu fero

Lollipop my toga lizard
Liguri lacertam quae sub toga mea vivit

Lip-read my trouser scroll
Lege labris volumen inguinale mihi

III
SERMO LATINUS ERUDITUS

ADVANCED LATIN

Useful Syntax
SYNTAXIS UTILIS

IMPERATIVE

Futue te ipsum
Go fuck yourself

IMPERFECT SUBJUNCTIVE
EXPRESSING A WISH FOR THE
PRESENT

Utinam tete futueres
Would that you would go fuck yourself

FIRST SUPINE EXPRESSING A WISH
FOR THE PRESENT WITH VERBS OF
MOTION

I fututum te ipsum
Go in order to fuck yourself

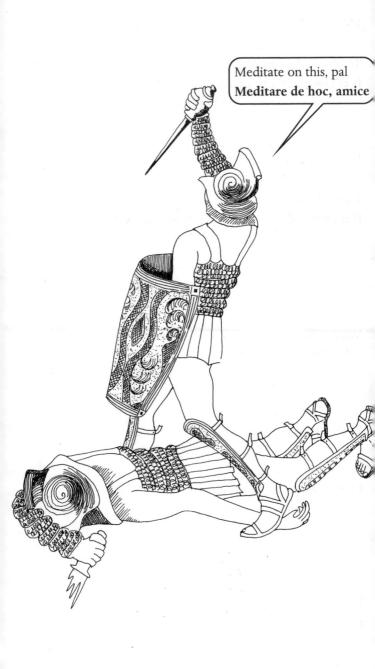

INFINITIVE WITH IMPERSONAL VERB

Te oportet futuere tete
It behooves you to go fuck yourself

PASSIVE PERIPHRASTIC

Tu tibi futuendus (futuendave) es
It is required of you to go fuck yourself

POTENTIAL SUBJUNCTIVE

Velim te futuas
I should like you to fuck yourself

SUBSTANTIVE CLAUSE OF PURPOSE

Te rogo ut futuas te ipsum
I beseech you to fuck yourself

GENITIVE OF PURPOSE

I tete futuendi gratia
Go for the sake of fucking yourself

FUTURE CONDITIONAL, LESS VIVID

Si te futuas, gaudeam
If you should go fuck yourself, I would rejoice

FUTURE CONDITIONAL, MORE VIVID

Se te futueris gaudebo
If you will have gone and fucked yourself, I will rejoice

PRESENT CONDITIONAL, CONTRARY TO FACT

Si te futueres, gauderem
If you were fucking yourself, I would be rejoicing

PAST CONDITIONAL, CONTRARY TO FACT

Se te futuisses, gavisus (gavisave) essem
If you had fucked yourself, I would have rejoiced

FUTURE PARTICIPLE DENOTING INTENTION OR LIKELIHOOD

Tete fututure, te saluto
You who are about to go fuck yourself, I salute you

FUTURE IMPERATIVE

Tete futuito
Make it your policy to fuck yourself

ABLATIVE ABSOLUTE

Te fututo, gaudeo
You having been fucked, I rejoice

. . . you often forget what you were going to say before you get to the verb

. . . saepe quid habeas in animo dicere priusquam ad verbum pervenias, obliviscaris

. . . you think only superstitious sissies are afraid of volcanoes

. . . credas molles superstitiosos solos timere montes Volcanios

. . . you can eat and have sex at the same time

. . . simul cenare et futuere possis

. . . you have ever used a chariot in a bar fight

. . . umquam in taberna curru proeliatus sis

. . . you never make major business decisions without first cutting open a sheep

. . . numquam de negotio magni momenti decernas sine extispicio

. . . your most recent domestic crisis was a slave revolt

. . . discrimen apud te recentissimum tumultus fuerit servilis

. . . you know anyone who married his own mother or
was raised by wolves

**. . . quempiam cognoscas qui matrem suam in
matrimonium duxerit vel sit a lupis alitus**

. . . you have a statue of yourself holding a sword in one
hand and the severed head of a Belgian in the other

**. . . possideas statuam tui, tenentem manu dextra
gladium, manu sinistra caput amputatum Belgae**

. . . you compliment the chef by throwing up

. . . coquum vomendo in mensam conlaudes

. . . you have a personal poisoner on your staff

. . . unus ex officialibus tuis propriis est venenarius

. . . the only vegetarian you ever met had hooves

. . . numquam phytophagis occurreris nisi ungulatis

. . . your idea of a party animal is a goat

. . . animal convivialissimum arbitreris esse caprum

. . . your car has sword blades welded to its wheels

. . . habeas currum falcatum

. . . there are usually about three hundred other people in
the tub when you take a bath

**. . . plerumque, cum laveris, adsint in calidario tecum
alii fere trecenti**

. . . you think it would be really cool to be Greek

. . . putes esse lepidissimum Graecari

. . . you stay home all day if you see a woodpecker over
your left shoulder or hear an owl

**. . . domi maneas totum diem cum post tergum
conspicias a sinistra picum, vel audias bubonem**

. . . you're never surprised to discover that the guy
running the empire is a moron, a pervert, or a lunatic

**. . . numquam admireris te invenire gubernatorem
imperii fatuum esse, vel pravum, vel vesanum**

Restaurant 'Tude
BILIS IN POPINA

My name is Sir – I'll be your customer tonight
Nomen mihi est Dominus – hodie vobiscum cenabo

My sign is, I sign the cheque
Natus sum signo signantis syngrapham

The only thing I wish to know about you is where the hell
you are when I want something
**De te scire volo solum ubi gentium sis cum alicuius
indigeam**

If those entrées are so special, why aren't they on the
menu?
**Si quidem illa fercula tantum praestant, cur in
epularum indice non sunt?**

Exactly how fresh is that pepper?
Quam recenter lectum est hoc piper?

Why do you put it in a mill the size of a war-trumpet?
Quamobrem id ponis in molina tanta quanta tuba est?

This is indeed a very impressive wine list, if you're in the mood for a bottle of grape-flavored rust remover that costs as much as a new sofa

Haec tabula vinorum grandia pollicetur cuicumque sit in animo bibere ex ampulla liquoris qui sapit uvas et solvit ferruginem et stat tanti quanti lectus novus

My compliments to the chef – the empire lost a truly inspired poisoner when he decided to go to cooking school

Summam coquo laudem tribuo – imperium venefico ingeniosissimo privatum est cum ille scholam coquinariam obire statuit

No dessert, thanks, unless it contains the antidote

Benigne, secundam mensam non requiro, nisi antidotum continet

I'd have written in a smaller tip but there is no Roman numeral for a penny

In syngrapha munusculum minus inscripsissem, sed non est littera Romana quae Ioachimici vicesimam significat

I'll be sure to recommend this place to my friends

Zago, zagas, zagat

Winespeak
DICTA ARBITRI VINI

It's an intense chalky white marked by overtones of
turpentine and lead, with a bright, long-lasting finish
**Vinum peralbum cretosum est, resinam terebinthinam
et cerussam redolens, nec sine polimine nitido
durabili**

It's a pointless little red wine with a unique balance of
ignorance and pretension made by an obnoxious
millionaire Napa Valley dilettante for self-important
dumb-lucky dickheads just like him
**Vinum irritum pusillum rubrum est, incomparabiliter
librans ignorantiam suam cum ostentatione, a
quodam Trimalchione Napaensi confectum salaputiis
gloriosis immerito fortunatis, persimilibus sui**

It's a dirt-cheap head-banging screw-top bum wine that I
poured into a leftover bottle with a fancy French label
while no one was looking
**Vappa vilissima est, quae capitis dolores facit, quamque
ex lagona obturamento versatili clausa in lagunculam
reliquam, cui pittacium Gallicum speciosum affixum
erat, transfudi, dum nemo me spectabat**

The Bestseller List
TABULA LIBRORUM VENDIBILISSIMORUM

Quick and Easy Decorating Secrets That Let You Turn a Rustic Hovel into a Charming Country Home without Busting Your Budget by Vitruvius

Artis Ornatus Arcana Per Quae Casa Tua Rustica Celeriter Expediteque Converti Potest in Villam Venustam Sine Sumptu Extra Modum Vitruvius Pollio scripsit

Eat Right – for that Lean and Hungry Look! by Cassius

Edi Recte – ut Speciem Macram et Ieiunam Geras auctore C. Cassio Longino

Great-Tasting Hot Meals Your Slaves Can Whip Up in Two Days or Less by Cato the Elder

Edulia Calida Sapidissimaque quae Familia Tua Potest Parare Duobus Diebus vel Uno M. Porcius Cato descripsit

Cleopatra's Hour-a-Day Bun-Firming Love-Muscle Sexercise Workout by Mark Antony

De Cleopatrae Callipygiana Exercitatione Aphrodisiaca Per Unam Horam in Singulos Dies Musculorum Venereorum M. Antonius scripsit

Letters to My Cat by Pliny the Younger
**Epistulae ad Felem Suam quas C. Plinius Caecilius
 Secundus scripsit**

What Colour is Your Catapult? by Frontinus
**Cuius Coloris est Catapulta Tua? Sextus Iulius
 Frontinus scripsit**

Oracles Say the Darnedest Things by Livy
**Oraculis Inusitatissima Enuntiantur Titus Livius
 scripsit**

Entrail Reading for Dummies by Cicero
Haruspicium Stipitibus Explicat M. Tullius Cicero

Men Are from Troy, Women Are from Greece by Virgil
**E Troia Viri, Ex Graecia Feminae Oriuntur P. Virgilius
 Maro scripsit**

*Now You Can Lose Weight without Vomiting with the
 Revolutionary Lark's Tongue Diet* by Apicius
**Nunc Adipem Deponere Potes Sine Vomitu per
 Diaetam Novam atque Inauditam Quae Linguarum
 Alaudarum Esum Praescribit L. Apicius scripsit**

Toujours, Gaul by Julius Caesar
Semper, Gallia C. Iulius Caesar scripsit

Latin for Trekkies
SERMO LATINUS
SECTATORIBUS
PEREGRINATIONIS ASTRALIS

Our shields are down to 25 per cent and those stupid
sparks are coming out of all the control panels!

**Scutorum nostrorum potestatis remanet solummodo
quarta pars, et istae scintillae ridiculae ex omnibus
claviaturis gubernatoriis evolant!**

We're being controlled by a subordinating conjunction of
time implying purpose or intent

**Coercemur coniunctione subiunctiva temporali quae
propositum vel intentionem significat**

Resistance is futile. Prepare to be assimilated into the
subjunctive.

**Resistere irritum est. Praeparate vos ad translationem
in modum subiunctivum.**

It's our only hope. Activate the transitive verbs and engage
the ablative of separation.

**Hoc sola spes nobis est. Verbis transitivis citis, adhibe
casum ablativum separationis.**

We're entering the future perfect indicative. We'll only
have one chance to achieve a case shift.

**Intramus tempus futurum perfectum modo indicativo.
Unam tantum occasionem habebimus mutandi
casum.**

We're slipping into the passive. Quick, reroute all available
power to the verb endings.

**In genus passivum labimur. Inmitte cito impetum
omnem quem in promptu habemus in terminationes
verborum.**

We have entered. We shall have entered! Do be entering!
Intravimus! Intraverimus! Intratote!

To be continued . . .
Narratio resumetur . . .

Attack Ads
PRAECONIUM PROCAX
CANDIDATORUM

Ask my opponent why he wants to put a tax on Bibles and
American flags to buy gourmet meals for convicted
murderers

**Quaerite a competitore meo cur vectigal Bibliis Sacris
et vexillis Americanis imponere velit ad epulas
comparandas homicidis condemnatis**

Call my opponent and demand that he stop accepting
campaign contributions from operators of nursing-
home casinos, publishers of pornographic children's
books, and owners of Mexican puppy mills

**Vocantes competitorem meum poscite ut desinat
accipere ad ambitionem alendam dona vel ab eis qui
virginibus puerisque libros edunt Sotadicos, vel ab eis
qui aleatoria in gerontocomiis apparant, vel ab eis qui
catellos in Hispania Nova immodice alunt**

Tell my opponent you oppose his plan to sponsor a law
forcing Sunday schools to hire unemployed bilingual
homosexual drug addicts

**Dicite competitori meo vos obstare proposito suo
ferendi legem quae cogat ludos Dominicales
conducere paedicatores otiosos bilingues
narcomaniacos**

Business Latin
SERMO LATINUS NEGOTIALIS

I respectfully decline to answer on the grounds that anything I might say would be a bald-faced lie
Recuso reverenter ne respondeam, quia quicquid dicam id sit mendacium impudens

It wasn't all done with smoke and mirrors – there were some bells and whistles, too
Non solum fumo speculisque, sed etiam tintinnabulis fistulisque factum est

It wasn't really a loss, it was a loan, which of course shows up as a profit
Non vero damnum erat sed mutuum, quod scilicet in rationibus existimatur lucrum

I was out of the loop, but I distinctly remember asking if it passed the smell test
Consilii particeps non eram, tamen memini clare me rogare num id insidias oleret

Due to an alien abduction, I have no recollection of anything else during that particular period of time
Quod raptus sum a transaetheriis, omnia quae evenerunt illo tempore de memoria mea exciderunt

I only sold my stock because a gypsy fortune-teller told me it was an unlucky month for any company with a vowel in its name

Omnes partes meas vendidi tantummodo eo, quod Aegyptia sortilega mihi dixit mensem infaustum esse cuiquam societati quae vocalem in nomine habet

Plus which, I needed cash to buy a condominium for my daughter's hamster

Mihi autem pecunia opus erat ad domicilium emendum criceto filiae meae

I mistook the shredder for a Xerox machine

Discissorem esse Xerographium perperam putavi

Look, let me off the hook and I will rat out every single person in the whole company

Age, da mihi veniam ac impunitatem, deferam unumquemque hominum in societate

Let the buyer go mad
FURAT EMPTOR

Ministerium consultatorium rerum technicarum tibi
gratias agit quod vocavisti
Thank you for calling tech support

Verisimile est te haudquaquam intellegere quod dicimus;
quid enim?
**You probably don't understand a word we're saying;
but so what?**

Vocatum tuum nullius momenti putamus eumque
neglegemus in ordine
**Your call is of no interest to us and will be ignored in
the order it was received**

Fieri potest ut vocatum tuum subauscultemus vel
transcribamus animi causa
**Your call may be monitored or recorded to provide us
with entertainment**

Omnes auxiliatores nostri nunc emptores alios
furiant
**All of our representatives are currently driving
other customers crazy**

Necesse tibi est morari circa tres dies et dimidiam
**Your approximate waiting time is three and one-half
days**

Preme gullulam primam uti musicam molestam audias
Press one to hear irritating music

Preme secundam ut sonum funis occupati audias
Press two to hear a busy signal

Preme tertiam uti tinnitum sempiternum lineae vacuae
audias
**Press three for the endless ringing of a non-working
extension**

Preme quartam uti statim disiungaris
Press four to be immediately disconnected

Sit iucundus tibi dies
Have a nice day

Jury Duty
OFFICIUM IUDICIALE

I'm hopelessly prejudiced – everyone in this court looks
like a criminal, including the judge

**Opinionem praeiudicatam immutabilem habeo –
omnes in hac basilica mihi videri nefarios esse,
praetore non excepto**

Not fair! Just last month I served as a hooded judge on a
secret military tribunal, but they made me promise not
to tell.

**Iniquum est! Modo proximo mense officio iudicis
cucullati functus sum in tribunali clandestino militari
tamen coactus sum iurare me de eo taciturum.**

I swear to tell the truth, the whole truth, and nothing but
the truth, so help, help me Rhonda

**Iuro sollemniter me dicturum verum, totum verum,
nihil praeter verum, ita me iuvet, iuvet Rhonda**

I think I can tell if someone is guilty just by looking at
them

**Credo me posse diiudicare utrum quis nocens an
innocens sit modo eum spectando**

If it's really, really close and the jury deadlocks, is it okay to flip a coin?

Si lis valde dubia sit, sententiis iuratorum paribus, liceatne nos nummum iactare, 'caput aut navem' enuntiantes?

If the guy is obviously guilty, can we just skip the trial and send him straight to prison under early admission?

Si reus manifesto sit in culpa, sitne fas nos quaestionem praetereuntes condemnatum in carcerem confestim conicere per admissionem subitariam?

If the gloves don't fit, do we have to acquit?

Si digitalia non congruant manibus, sitne nobis necesse reum absolvere?

Does the jury room have a minibar?

Estne cubiculum deliberationis instructum cistula potionum spirituosarum?

I believe the minimum award in civil cases should be one million dollars, but if you lose, you get the electric chair

Mea sententia, causam privatam obtinenti ut minimum decies centena milia Ioachimicorum addici debent, at de perdente supplicium ultimum in electrica sella sumendum est

I plan to find everyone not guilty by reason of I am extremely pissed off

In animo mihi est, iracundiae meae maximae causa, quemque reum absolvere de crimine

But in a larger sense, can any of us say that we are truly
innocent?

**Quod autem ad res universas attinet, ecquis nostrum
dicere potest se vere innocentem esse?**

No, no! It was me! It was me all along! I did it! I did it and
I'm glad! Ha-ha, just kidding.

**Minime! Non est! Ego fui! Semper ego! Ego facinus feci!
Atque gaudeo me fecisse! Hahahae! Tantummodo
iocabar.**

Stealth Latin
SERMO LATINUS CLANDESTINUS

What you say in Latin
What you say it means
What it really means

Stupra fascino volanti torum pistrinum provolventem
You never cease to amaze me with your deeply insightful remarks
Go take a flying fuck at a rolling doughnut

Quin futuis uxorem tuam foedam?
Why doesn't everyone recognize your genius?
Why don't you go screw your ugly wife?

Velim caput tuum devellere deinde in confinium gulae cacare
I just want to tell you how much I appreciate your constructive criticism
I'd like to rip off your head and take a dump in the hole

Mande merdam et morere
Keep up the good work
Eat shit and die

Propudium parcissimum
I'll get the cheque
You cheap bastard

Carrus exsecrabilis est! Venditor te irrumavit!
What a great car! You got a heck of a deal!
What a piece of shit! You got taken to the cleaners!

Aspice hanc supellectilem vilem. Quale gurgustium est.
Fabulous house – I love your taste.
Look at this cheesy crap. What a dump.

Rotaturne capitulum huius, virus exspuens viride?
Well, now, really, isn't that the cutest baby you've ever
seen?
Does its head spin around and spit green slime?

**Amica tua est originis extraterrestrialis. Si fortuna tibi
faveat, cum astronavem suam ista refecerit, a terra
tuaque vita discedet tam cito quam fulmen ascendit.**
Your girlfriend is a knockout. Talent, beauty, brains – she
has it all.
*She's a space alien. If you're lucky, when she gets her flying
saucer fixed, she'll be out of here and out of your life in a
flash.*

**Amicus tuus expers rationis est. Viculus nescioquis
barone suo privatus est.**
Your boyfriend is a great guy. No wonder you've been
keeping him to yourself.
*He's a total moron. Somewhere there's a village missing its
idiot.*

Speciem scurrae habes. Spectaculum petauristarum bestiarumque nescieGam adesse.

Dynamite outfit! It really looks good on you.

You look like a clown. I didn't know the circus was in town.

Stealth Latin for Golfers
SERMO LATINUS CLANDESTINUS IN LUSU CALEDONIO

Quod fustuarium!
Nice swing!
What a hack!

Salaputium fortunatum!
Great shot!
You lucky fuckhead.

Seligatur clava imprudenter
Be the right club.
Be the wrong club.

Pilula, curre in harenariam et defode te.
Hurry up ball, get some air! Be there!
Get in that bunker and bury.

Vola! Aberra! Egredere praeter terminos!
Stop! Hit something! Stay in play!
Go! Get lost, ball! Go out of bounds!

Immerge te in aquam!
Stay dry!
Get wet!

Decurre ab area leni in gramen densum!
Sit down! Bite!
Run off the green into the rough!

Transili puteolum!
Go in the hole!
Lip out!

Euax!
Aww, too bad!
Hurray!

Bad Latin, the Dirty Dozen

SERMO LATINUS IMPUDICUS: DUODECIM OBSCENA

asshole	*culus, i* m.; *podex, podicis,* m.
balls	*coleus, i* m.;
to be blown & to blow	*irrumo, irrumare* *fello, fellare;* *ligurio, ire;* *(verpam) comedo, esse, edi, estum*
to bugger	*pedico, are*
butt	*clunis, is* m. & f. *(clunes, ium);* *natis, is* f. *(nates, ium);* *puta, ae* f.
cock	*capulus, i* m.; *cauda, ae* f.; *cicer, is* n.; *clavus, i* m.; *cucumis, eris* m.; *falcula, ae* f.; *fascinum, i* n.; *gladius, i* m.; *hasta, ae* f.; *membrum, i* n.;

mentula, ae f.;
peculium, i n.;
radix, icis, f.;
rutabulum, i n.;
sicula, ae f.;
telum, i n.;
verpa, ae f.;
vomer, eris m.

cunt *aratiuncula, ae* f.;
cunnus, i m.

fart, to fart *crepitus, us.* m.:
strepitus, us m.;
crepo, crepare, crepui, crepitum;
pedo, pedere, pepedi, peditum;
strepito, are

to fuck *concumbo, concumbere, concubui, concubitum;*
futuo, futuere, futui, fututum

to jerk off *frico, fricare, fricui, frictum (fricatum);*
percieo, ire, ivi, itum;
sollicito, are;
tero, terere, trivi, tritum;
tracto, tractare

piss, to piss *urina, ae* f.;
meio, meiere, mixi, mictum;
mingo, mingere, minxi, minctum

shit, to shit *fimus, i* m. & *filmus, i* n.;
merda, ae f.;
stercus, oris n.;
caco, are